Sometimes Words Appear Easily On A Page

Poetry By James R. Ellerston and the Contributions of Others

JAMES RAY ELLERSTON
302 Lincoln St., Pella, IA 50219
jrellerston@gmail.com
(515) 570-2052

Copyright © 2023 James R. Ellerston

All rights reserved. No part of this publication may be reproduced, distributed, or transmitted in any form or by any means, including photocopying, recording, or other electronic or mechanical methods, without the prior written permission of the publisher.

First paperback edition January 2022.

ISBN: 979-8873256747

Printed in the United States of America.

Some Words Appear Easily

It is when these few well chosen words,
written down in haste on pages in past years,
that recorded the happenings and emotions felt
about critical times in the long history of mankind,
and great events that occurred in our own individual lives,
which were long enduring in the recesses of the mind--
and when given a free moment
sprang forth somewhat in disarray,
and were scribbled down
to be later repeatedly carefully edited,
until they were finally existing as an enduring poem
upon a printed page.

James R. Ellerston
February 15, 2023

Writing Your Own Poetry

One should write to express beauty and joy. It is possible to let-out feelings of inner pain, trauma, or grief. One can express the inner-self in a form where only poetry can be the medium.

We may have emotion about a historical moment, and capture that moment in verbal form. We may be challenged to use found material to convey a new honesty to a new audience, to use words to project a photograph, to tell a truth. As a poet we have a responsibility to convey only truths to the world-- to tell the truth about historical happenings that have been simplified or rewritten as propaganda.

Poets should convey their honesty to a new audience, and motivate people to a purpose in their lives. Describing beauty may help others to open their eyes and see it too. Telling of another's pain may motivate others to make a difference in the world.

The barriers of metrical feet, or standard forms, or using rhyme may discourage people from using their voice.

Write it, do not judge it, save it, edit it later, maybe share for suggestions; then polish your final draft. Share it with persons with whom you are comfortable or with the populations of this Earth.

The Author and Poet

James Ellerston, born in 1950, is a poet, historian, musician, father and husband, who as author-editor, with this volume is putting-out his fourteenth self-published collection of poetry. He was a music educator for forty years in Iowa, and still is performing on violin and viola in community ensembles.
He earned a B.A. from Central College (Pella, Iowa) in 1972, an M.S. in Education from Bemidji State University (Bemidji, Minnesota) in 1976, and an additional B.A. in Management and Personnel from Buena Vista University (Storm Lake, Iowa) in 1987.

He has traveled extensively, nine times to Europe, as well as western Canada and the United States, including Hawaii, and driving with his wife and children to and from Alaska.

He grew up on a farm in northern Iowa, lived in Fort Dodge, Iowa for 45 years, and spent part of each summer for 66 years at a cabin on Ten Mile Lake near Hackensack, Minnesota. Time in summers is also spent at a cabin of his wife's family, in a forest region near Medford, Wisconsin.

Since the fall of 2016 he has resided in Pella, Iowa with wife Shelley. His son also lives in Pella. He spends periods of time with his daughter and her family, with his two grandsons, of Salt Lake City, Utah.

The family dog is currently a Jack Russell Terrier named "Bravo".

Sometimes Words Appear Easily On A Page

Title Page
Some Words Appear Easily
Writing Your Own Poetry
The Author and Poet
Table Of Contents: Sometimes Words Appear Easily On A Page
Contributors and Givers of Inspiration

End Of Summer Leisure
Passing A Minnesota Day Away
Diary: It's A Cold Last Wednesday In September At Ten Mile Lake

Boyhood Gone
Did No One Suggest Book Bags For Carrying Lifetime Memories?
Memories Brought From Their Rightful Hiding Places

Back In Iowa For Fall And Winter Days
Never Got His Name
Stuff Just Goes Wrong Always by John Bowman
May Seeing Sunsets Help Us
At Howell Station, Red Rock Lake
This Splendid Day Happened Upon Us
Now I've Seen These Pictures Of Our Room

A New Year
A Musician's Northern Iowa Sojurns
And I Want To Hear From You
Sorting Receipts Again
It's Pretty
A Place You've Once Been
A Clouded-Over Monday Morning In January
Massed Gun Violence

Poems From My Daughter's Teenage Years
Me
After A Summer's Rain
Night On The Lake
Piano Sonata
Freezer Burn
Looking To The Future

**Didn't Desire A *Rumspringa*
But Searched For A Pella Of The Mind**
    I.   I grew up on a farm
    II.   In 1967 Central College hosted Dr. Martin Luther King
    III. In the summer of 1967 my mother attended a French
    IV. Later that fall the nation saw the assassination
    V.   In the middle of my high school senior year, I turned 18
    VI. In my own idealized life
    VII. In the fall of 1968 I became a college student
    VIII. By spring guy's hair was unkempt and long
    IX. The summer of 1969 I returned home to the farm
    X.   On Dec. 1, 1969, our safe student-deferred-cocoon
    XI. But as the war killing dragged on--
    XII. In my senior year at Central and planning afterward
    XIII. In my first job after graduation from Central
    XIV. Six years ago my wife and I moved from the city

Brisk Winter Days With Dark Nights
The Morning After That Night I Knew I'd Heard Talent
The Last Corn Shelling On That Farm
While On A Sunny Afternoon I Walked
Just A Thought On A Monday
The Wonders In Our Worlds Of Memory
Memories Of Watery Places Over Time
I have so many words by Stefan Crowl
Last Look Around A House Of Past Memories

Spring Flowers Grew And Ideas Bloomed
The Flag Was Pulled Down And I Questioned Our Lives
On A Walk Together
With Grandpa's Microscope
Around The Campus
Given Yet Another Chance For My Heart To Go On
He Spoke At The Tulip Tower May 8, 1970
Written For Widowers, Everyone

Boston In Springtime
Boston In The Spring (May 9-14, 2023)
      I. Our weather was always sunny
      II. A chair-filled stage was well lit
      III. As our five days in the Boston area
      IV. People must have been shorter back then
      V. The Navy base had the USS Cassin Young
      VI. The Warren Tavern in Charleston
      VII. A late afternoon trip was made
      VIII. We experienced six tourist days
      IX. Our connecting flight home
      X. After our longer second flight

Wisconsin Cabin Opened-Up Lives
For A Dear Young Friend
After Another Year: A 2023 Trip To See My Wisconsin Friends
      I. know they live in a world of long hours
      II. I had followed a red pickup that afternoon
      III. I drove miles of challenging dusty country
      IV. We traveled next to our own lakeside home
      V. Once more now, at age 73
      VI. Thoughtlessly Distanced
      VII. So Briefly In An Open-Armed Hug
      VIII. Homeward Bound

At A Minnesota Lake For A Summer Of Fun
Smoke Again In 2023
Not Really Out Of The Woods Yet
Today
Bryce's 8th Birthday
With A Hot Coffee Prelude
Summer Solstice
Morning Meditation
Turtle Town Art Fair
Another Saturday July 1st

Mid-Summer Good Times
On Nature's Travels
Annual Boat Parade 10:00 AM, 4th Of July, 2023
The Morning Of July 6, 2023
The Music Will Go On
Being In This Lake Stays With You
They Played Together At Ten Mile Lake
Afloat With Liam And Bryce (Tuesday July 18, 2023)
Child Of Edinburg, Texas in 1939
When The Car Had Driven Down The Lane
Shadows of Days They Left Behind
A Great Day Begins
Forever (by Stefan Crowl)
Big Waves Crashing In The Storm
Between Lake And Lawn
A Wee Song With Singing Smiles
From Glenn's Photos He Took While Traveling
Toddler's Final Journey On Governor Abbott's Orders
Song For Alan (Takatsuka)
We Are Warned Of Cold That's Coming
Feed And Water Daily
Doing Dishes
Fall Bombing From Oak Trees
Last Mid-afternoon Visit With Shirley 2023
Lending Libraries
On My Nearly Empty Lakeside Street
On Friday September 22, 2023
My Last Saturday On Our Shore For 2023

In Pella For A Fun Week
Joe Played Wonderfully At Alumni Pans

More Poems From My Daughter's Teenage Years
Peace
Wake
Where Raindrops Fall
Old Glory
Daydream

Fall October Trip To Thomat In Wisconsin
View On A Rainy October Day
Our Saturday Morning In Wisconsin
The Dog Wanted Out Again
That Day At Thomat
Photogenic
Last Evening's Supper
In The Night

A Grove Of Tree Poems
- I. What is it about a Sycamore
- II. A Banyan Tree grew on Maui
- III. Between our two Wisconsin cabins
- IV. Only in one city
- V. Outside my Iowa farmhouse
- VI. The city had cut those
- VII. Roads diverged as we drove
- VIII. After hours of driving southward
- IX. We'd gone and played outdoors together
- X. My wife and I had lived in our house

We Returned To Pella For The Fall
Met Central College Friends That Afternoon
Scenes Of Fall In Glenn's Photos
Seasonal Changes in Small Town Iowa
Mideast War Games Again
Gift Of A Watermelon
Thoughts About When I Walked On A Saturday Afternoon

A Morning Phone Call
It Didn't Always Mean Something When She Nodded
"What Sweeter Music" Could Have Reached One's Ears
In A Tuesday Afternoon Rehearsal

Somme: WWI Poems From Letters I. - XII.
    I. Just as dawn was breaking the 2nd of July
    II. The third day I was exhausted
    III. We were wondering what we could do
    IV. We are right back in a place
    V. There was comfort in coming straight from the trenches
    VI. The battalion was withdrawn to a camp after many days
    VII. What silly details my letters must seem
    VIII. Someone was asking if there was to be a sort of Christmas
    IX. The last evening being cold, innumerable small fires
    X. Later in the morning we Suffolks had been moved forward
    XI. As a battalion, we tramped the old duckboards again
    XII. This 16th of January the cold is intense

Thanksgiving For Fall Harvest Done
Five November Happenings
His Harvest of 2023 Corn Completed
After The Fall Harvest
Moving Toward Thanksgiving
Sixty Years Afterward There Is No Debate About Some Facts
I Mourned With Ireland

Contributors and Givers of Inspiration

James Ellerston
Glenn Henriksen
John Bowman
Stefan Crowl
James Rasmussen
Steve Masimore
Stephen Covey
Jim DeSmidt
Sherril Graham
Sue Wilson
Shirley Ohrtman
Charly Hertel
La Vonne Tow
Linda Thompson
John Cassidy
The New Yorker online
Belva Ramler Henrickson
Bret Crowl
Ezra Blasi
Common Ground at Central College
Dr. Ken Weller
John Keats
Jim Metzger
Dr. Julia Ellerston
Nick Avery Ludwig
Austin Olson
Brok Hathaway
Michael Andreas Häringer
Daeren F. Harp
Bryce A Romanelli-Gobbi
Liam E. Romanelli-Gobbi

Russell Lee
NBC News
Alan Takatsuka
Debby Takatsuka
Shirley Miller
Joe Roberts
Efrain Garcia
Marge Gale
Jane Matteson
Shelley Best Ellerston
Kris DeWild
Christopher M. Ellerston
AI Program Chat GPT
Central College A Cappella Choir
Brad Lampe
Dominic Sexton
Richard van Emden
Sara Vriesen
Mark Orabinoski
Carol and Dave Platt
Kama Ibsen
Abandoned Iowa Project
My Jack Russell Terrier dog 'Bravo'
Brian Hart
ALMA of Central College Music Department
Keegan Joel VanDevender for Finishing and Publishing

End Of Summer Leisure

Passing A Minnesota Day Away

Thursday had been another gray shadowed day
but was followed by emerging sunshine in late afternoon
encouraging me to take a brief pre-dinner swim to bathe
for refreshment and cleanliness in a cooling-off lake--
chilling waters dropping warmth each day in temperature degrees
as the numbers on the September calendar got higher
now that I'm in my last three weeks at our summer cabin.

A prolonged beautiful sunset extended my daily joy with its
soft lavender hues replacing the usual sky of Hamm's blue waters;
the first distant shining white ripples on a nearly calm surface were
followed by a golden sphere at the altitude of western smoke with
a return to a a bright silver stream of light moving upon the lake,
and a coda of a descending fiery red ball and heavens cloud filled
with floating orangeness for a final cadence above the far shore.

Hours of velvet blackness blanketed my sleep-filled night
while a gentle patter of rain danced away for hours upon the roof.

James R. Ellerston
September 16, 2022

Diary: It's A Cold Last Wednesday In September
At Ten Mile Lake

At dawn's early breaking light it was our coldest morning yet;
the early western cloudless sky was a rosy hue above
with heavens' pink reflected on lake's flat un-waved surface;
thick vaporous white clouds were rising from its calmness;
in sunrise hours it continued losing the warmth of its stored heat;
what had enabled many pleasant summer swims to be long,
this cold morning boiling away, on a near frost-temperature morning
robbing comfort from any last swim or any tuneful September song.

I gazed through the cozy closed external windows of double pane,
but felt my own internal pain at making preparation for leaving--
a regretful emotion occurring with an empty loneliness,
at a seasonal farewell to neighbors and friends from states distant;
I did tasks and labor to close-up the cabin for winter's safety,
while putting boats, beach chairs and toys for summer fun away
stored safely inside until next year's arrival day when all comes out,
when it's another period of grandchildren's energetic vacation play.

In this final busy week of packing-up and needed repairs,
trying to clean things correctly and make all circumspect--
I had tried to fix a hot water heater with new parts and self-dares,
but without any success I was disappointed in my work;
I should have bought more trial parts at the local hardware store;
if there'd been a chance to enjoy those last days with self-respect
I needed to get the heater fixed to have a hot-shower again inside,
yet for many months it will all stand empty with no one to inspect.

James R. Ellerston
September 28, 2022
Revised October 5, 2022

Boyhood Gone

Did No One Suggest Book Bags For Carrying Lifetime Memories?

He would walk that paved State Highway 43 edge alone
from his story and a half white house on the gradually curved street,
where as Cub Scouts we had gathered in neighbors unfinished basements,
and moving at that time past the tallest concrete grain silo in the state
arriving in two blocks of businesses and at the storefront City Library.

It was a Danish immigrant farm town world,
and celebrates that ethnic heritage with flying flags yet today;
just another Iowa elevator town on miles of rural connecting railroad
which once conveyed an abundance of farm field grain--
now hauled by highway-clogging trucks, the tracks all torn up and gone.

Ringsted was a complete village, with movie theater, stores, and schools;
two Lutheran churches preached Sunday mornings-- one in Danish language;
his family and mine and others attended the same Presbyterian church,
first a white wooden building standing by a country school for Sunday school,
later in a newer red brick colonial style built around my age of ten.

The city librarian lived across the street from our elementary playground,
and while using the swings we suspiciously eyed her house;
you later expressed that she didn't keep-up with books,
and that your mom was on the library board,
and new books moved through your house on the way to the library.

I lived on a farm nine miles out in the country; my library was in our home;
I rarely used a library-- we had shelves of books throughout our house;
my great-aunt kept us gifted with new award-winning children's books;
you went most Wednesdays and Saturdays to the Ringsted Library,
often walking home carrying books stacked precariously up to your chin.

You hold memories of the wide green cloth library tape
repairing bindings on most of the Bobseys, Nancys, and Hardys
at that time original editions, or so we suspect now;
you read them repeatedly by yourself;
I remember hearing our teacher read Bobseys To The Seashore to our class.

While we were in grade school the town of Ringsted was a thriving place--
three churches, its own High School, newspaper, doctor, telephone company,
red-roofed water tower, city park with war memorials, two hardware stores,
two groceries, two restaurants, two filling stations with repair bays, a tavern;
red, green, and yellow farm implements all had local dealers who did repairs.

Today there is still a functioning branch bank, and a Library there and open;
the school district, one proudly independent is consolidated over a wide area;
1950's and 1960's Ringsted was another world, and you have commented,
it has not been an evolution but a devolution; yet community spirit is strong;
while some physical structure is gone, there is still a local grocery store.

We grew up in an era of family, church, school, and community spirit;
and for us the Boy Scouts helped us grow and thrive in those years;
many thanks to parents like yours who let our Cub den and troop meetings;
Boy Scouts often met in the white wooden Opera House, now demolished.
In basements and in churches, has our Troop 61 BSA lived on?

Today one can browse on the Internet the Ringsted Dispatch archives,
which some intermittently do; one might enjoy the social news--
lots of visiting was reported in newspapers of that era; school news is fun;
Ringsted, and small schools, had girls athletics long before Titled mandates;
six-on-six girls basketball packed the local gym on winter nights.

It's good getting December cards to share and sort our thoughts and views,
and though classmates are spread out from Iowa to Maine and California,
we can focus on memories of a town not its former self, but not a ghost--
today two churches still fill with Sunday's faithful worshiping throngs,
but school students have a new mascot, and now sing a different song.

James R. Ellerston
December 14, 2022
Suggested by a Christmas Card from John (and Laurie) Phillips mailed December 6, 2022. We were friends, fellow students, and both Boy Scouts in the troop both his parents helped lead until they moved away from our town.
Other building stores omitted in the poem are the Thomas Department Store, which sold dry goods and furniture, the post office, barber shop, and Lund Drug store where I purchased my first Superman comic books.

Memories Brought From Their Rightful Hiding Places

Ringsted grade school K-6, was in a previous high school of brown brick;
a narrow upper floor hallway haunted by matted class year picture groupings,
had individual graduate's photos hung high on walls staring downward at us
above rows of coat hooks on oak boards between doors to classrooms;
longtime teachers were Mrs. Holte and Mrs. Kearns;
newcomers were Miss Fisher (later Mrs. Benson) and Mr. Pringle.

West of the hopscotch sidewalk was a block of family homes in a row,
and in one lived a Great Dane serving as mascot for the schools;
the dog ventured across the street stealing hats, jackets, and ball gloves;
our classmate Craig, who was known to the dog,
would leave the school property after asking permission,
and return the stolen items to the often-terrified children.

Music was strong in the Ringsted community, schools, and churches;
summer band concerts were Saturday nights "uptown";
our music room was behind the school in a Quonset hut;
it was a pleasant room, but detached from the main building
reached via the school kitchen, through the furnace room door,
up a short stretch of stairs, and more steps in outdoor weather.

Behind the school, was a playground and a softball diamond,
with muddy bases and wire mesh screening behind home plate;
playground equipment of the era provided fun and dangers,
time on wooden swings, a metal slide, a merry-go-round,
and climbing adventurous although dangerous "monkey-bars";
a coded series of bells signaled ends of recess periods.

Iowa winters held fascinations and weather challenges;
Mr. Cronk and noisy steam-heated iron radiators kept us warm and cozy;
their hot tops laid-out with wet mittens, cotton gloves, and scarves;
all this damp fabric drying gave classrooms the "smell of wet sheep";
a jumble of overshoes was piled-up at the doors of the building,
and often sorted-out by names penned inside the boots' tops.

The kitchen-lunchroom became our 1st grade room, with Mrs. Moore;
the platform stage was converted into steps up to a hot lunch kitchen;
new folding tables equipped the small gymnasium floor as a lunch room,
players stood with backs against brick walls when inbounding the basketball
to avoid being "over the line", but had fun;
passes thrown too high would often hit the glaring overhead lights.

What had once been my 3rd grade classroom, became our school's library;
like schools across the United States we gathered attentively in the gym
and seated on the floor watched with interest the launch of the Space Race
in its early episodes on a single black and white television;
later after standing empty, our beloved Ringsted grade school,
a town landmark for many years, succumbed to a fatal fire.

James R. Ellerston
February 17-18, 2023
Inspired by an email of James Rasmussen January 8, 2023

Back In Iowa
For Fall And Winter Days

Never Got His Name

Who was the freshman kinesiology major who wants to teach P.E.,
and waited in Weller on Wednesday December 14 for his friend
who was finishing his semester exam;
but this guy listened attentively and so patiently
in my hour of need and grief,
to me rambling on about my student
on the anniversary of the day he died (December 15, 2020);
I remember he was a football player and played "safety";
he had dark wavy hair, told me he weighed 185 pounds, was 6'1";
I want to thank him for being so kind
but I never got his name.

James R. Ellerston
December 15, 2022

Stuff Just Goes Wrong Always

It's people who are afraid,
who hurt as a verb;
those who have been hurt the most
become the most afraid.

So here's my holding on with my fear,
and white knuckles to my relationships;
yet someone not feeling a thing
is what I encounter.

I squeezed so tightly,
the fear hurt only me;
I attract narcissists,
I'm perfect food.

Everything romantic that happened to me,
would make an amazingly emotional memoir;
all the conversations that I didn't notice
that I was left in for months.

I've gone for two years on alone in the end,
without noticing there were no replies;
but reminded that I was always worthy of being loved,
I am unsure-- how the people I dated seemed to disagree.

Stuff just goes wrong always,
it's abruptly usually that I'm put in pain;
having a memory-- thinking about all the good times
it's hard to believe it has been so long.

John Bowman on Messenger December 20, 2022
John Bowman Facebook post December 11, 2022
Edited James R. Ellerston December 21, 2022

May Seeing Sunsets Help Us

"Strength lies in differences,
not in similarities", someone said;
"One of these things
is not like the others",
he once typed above photographs--
and showed five of them, all sunsets;
four were reflected on calm water,
one above snow on a frozen lake's surface;
the same two chairs shown in all five pictures
with no one in them, both empty,
yet waiting to be filled, by two still alone.

These hues of color amid the clouds
enrich my worldly dreams
of beauty in all my passing hours;
from the start of life until the finality
of quiet darkness at day's end;
after the teasing and torment
and throughout my struggles
may reddening light ease my mind
and ease my sleep until the end of time;
but at the end of a Christmas day
may sunsets warm our hearts sending us on our merry way.

James R. Ellerston
December 26, 2022
Based on a Facebook post by Steve Masimore Dec. 18, 2022
Quotation of line by Stephen Covey in Fb post by Steve Masimore
Paraphrase of Facebook line by Jim DeSmidt December 25, 2022

At Howell Station, Red Rock Lake

It was a breezy eight degrees,
so we didn't stay long.
The Canada Geese didn't mind the cold,
or seem to notice
while honking out a little songful music.
After landing on a calm surface,
a few more later coming,
were seen as dark shadows on rippling water,
within snow-covered banks,
beneath skeletons of dark bare trees
reaching for the skies above.
Crescent moons, so delicate and lovely,
are a favorite on clear blue evenings.

James R. Ellerston
December 28, 2022
Sherril Graham a Facebook post and pictures on Dec. 26, 2022
Red Rock Lake- a reservoir on the Des Moines River near Pella, Ia.

This Splendid Day Happened Upon Us

This wonderful day of late December unusual warmth,
freed me from the imprisonment of being trapped indoors,
from an internal exile confined within my house by bitter cold--
since going bundled-up to church on the Eve of Christmas;
I could finally again venture out, walk about, and bask in sunshine.

Snow drifts melted upon grass lawns turned into riverlets,
trickling water pooled on lower places into sidewalk ponds,
which I carefully stepped around to keep shoes dry;
a stronger breeze blew and I buttoned up my jacket;
flags flew noisily straight out from their poles, held by wind's wrath.

It's magnificent on these intermittent thawing days
to see the blue of a near-cloudless sky above,
and feel the warmth of midafternoon rays upon our flesh;
on this occurrence of near-record temperatures in Iowa,
I celebrated my physical health by strolling familiar concrete paths.

I saw only one lone college student traveling on a strengthening quest
with beautiful youthful running form striding his distance to a goal;
he was probably off to the gym or track to celebrate fleeting youthful years
that soon will pass and sundown into his middle aged responsibilities;
for now he knows enough to enjoy this sunshine period amid life's storms.

So with some carefully chosen illustrative verbal elements,
I have carefully drawn this joyful winter-thaw picture
of beauty found in rapidly melting snow and nearly absent ice;
bare sidewalks were once again safe to trod, so I walked briskly;
a fast pace sped me on my way, the motive exercise-- my adult play.

James R. Ellerston
December 29, 2022

Now I've Seen These Pictures Of Our Room

I'm reminded that while others also worked there amid the years,
    found places elsewhere, moved to different jobs and cities,
this had been a hallowed hall of great personalities, the dedicated
    who were the baton wielders who staged their craft therein;
silent yet painless demonstrations of snare drum rolls
    could be executed upon one's palm
by a Master at percussion named Arnold, one of a kind,
    the first University of Michigan alum to major in timpani;
and a versatile violinist who taught orchestra and other areas,
    even electric guitar in a long career in the room;
there was a Luther College grad who brought a competitive desire
    to marching band performance in the junior high era;
then a clarinet virtuoso educated at Drake University, an expert at
    motivating sixth graders-- in her element in the middle school;
and a patient enduring young Central College grad taught younger
    students in the band and thrived in her Fair Oaks years.

Now these pictures of desolation fill the screen before me,
    clouding my memory of those good times;
they have not spread happiness throughout my soul for this place
    where I worked with so many others I grew to love
over three and a half decades of my teaching career,
    making music with students in their awkward growing years;
I was privileged sharing these spaces with gifted staff members;
    our room now appears in a state of ruinous desecration--
vandals, time, and neglect have undone the readiness
    of this entire school building for teaching,
for conveying the love of melodious sound and feelings of joy that
    were once shared within these well constructed walls.

In these recent photos sunlight brightly streams through windows,
      my office door still stands open in welcoming greeting;
but the blue carpet shows years of wear, water stains,
      and wavy ripples across the floor,
where litter and fallen ceiling tiles lie scattered about,
      from cumulative effects of leaking roof maintenance deferred;
no freshening air flows through HVAC tubes hanging angling down
      where ceiling vents once hung spaced out;
there is no longer purpose to the closets of empty shelves
      once filled with cherished student musical instruments;
now no one practices tuneful melodies here within these walls
      with their rows of acoustic tiles in such disarray;
the music making is now silent, the concerts are over,
      the teachers and students are gone;
those who once banded together have gone away, march to their
      own drums, and have abandoned those memorable times.

James R. Ellerston
December 31, 2022

Pictures were from the post of The Abandoned Iowa Project of a building now known as Fair Oaks School. "Built in 1931, this expansive school building has gone by many names throughout its 90 year existence... attending classes under the banner of Fair Oaks, South Junior High School, and Duncombe Elementary. Multiple additions were added throughout its life time.... Fair Oaks closed its doors for good in 2015.... fallen into disrepair. Copper thieves, vandals, and unchecked environmental damage have wreaked havoc on the building in the seven years since its closure." The site includes almost forty pictures showing damage. The building is in Fort Dodge, Iowa.

A New Year

I have a birthday,
and am a year older;
it's a new start;
many resolve to do better.

A Musician's Northern Iowa Sojurns

These miles of wintery road he urgently and timely travels
between the flat sleeping fields laid fallow for months of rest;
he goes without complaints on these parallel bands of ice and white
bringing music to share with its abundant joys and his personal insights
from one small town church to another for services and final rites,
or to a caring home for aged people in life's declining fights.

Through narrow passages where plows cast mounds strongly aside
freeing paths of asphalt and concrete on which to safely steer,
he drives where vast sculptured snow piled high and drifts abound;
he traverses many treacherous miles to spread melodious songs' sound
by routinely playing piano keys on a variety of varied instruments he's found,
keeping spirits high in flat northwest Iowa-- making some glad to be around.

All these vistas viewed were captured by an artful eye with a cell phone lens
showing rural country and small town life and a past which once had been;
stalwart farm groves darkly outline many a distant horizon's view,
where early-rising farm families filled their days with a chore or two;
with heavy storms there are sidewalks to shovel and streets to plow through;
inside cozy houses families read, play games, find something together to do.

There were birds that lingered in their chilly bare-branched cold homes,
or scurried across frozen lawns or sheltered from snowflakes on towering trunks;
at night it's a sight seeing icy boughs shimmer from light of a full moon;
the crackling ice coating of the trees isn't thawing anytime soon;
school was canceled again, so that morning through a drift a tunnel was hewn;
two young boys built a fort before the meal of ancestral Danish recipes at noon.

Wind eroded soil streaked clean snowscapes-- a reminder of our chosen path--
controllable by planting windbreaks, cover crops, or tillage techniques;
there is a beauty where lakes and marsh are mixed with rich fertile land,
wooded areas are preserved in parks where crafted stone shelters stand,
as sheltered picnic areas and beaches remain of gently sloping clean sand;
life here mixes work, play, and joy found by giving a neighbor a helping hand.

James R. Ellerston
January 7, 2023
Facebook posts of Glenn Henriksen the week of January 1-7, 2023

And I Want To Hear From You

And I want to hear from you in your room of solitude
and listen as you play loudly on a guitar for hours
and you direct fingers to hold down strings resounding
and as they'll form a chord beneath your struggling efforts
and you boldly strum hurt feelings sounding and filling space
and you hit the strings over and over in a pattern
and let out the anger that you cannot otherwise voice
and wish you could make a song releasing out your pain
and realize you could turn to a new page in the instruction book
and try another chord with your good hearted melody
and your gagged voice could find the expressive words.

And I want to hear from you in your room of solitude
and as you try out different lively harmonies back and forth
and over and over alternately hear lively melodic suggestions they make
and realize with the another chord there'll be a song worth singing
and will eagerly look ahead and turn the next page
and you have ideas and poetry to offer freely to the world
and try to say something to help you through the darkened hours
and not that life's roses are red and violets are not
and risk saying something that's real this time and a chance for you
and you know already that you are blue and realize that truth
and have forgotten you're worthy of the love others have for you

And I want to hear from you in your room of solitude
and you must hang on to these chords you've been given today
and make them last a little longer, a few more beats and days
and soon you'll find another harmonious progression
and find a way to offer up your verse to the eternally twinkling stars
and try to go on until your lifetime's hours lighten in the morning
and restful sleep has cleansed your mind of vengeful thoughts
and you hopefully wake to face a new dawn of continued growth
and give yourself a chance to flower in the garden of opportunities
and because for you it isn't autumn yet in the seasons of your life
and it's no time to slumber and just wither on the vine
and in the temporary cold, betray the promise of the coming spring.

James R. Ellerston   January 11, 2023

Sorting Receipts Again

It's now that time of the new calendar year's beginning
that we sort and sift through the boxes of tattered receipts--
these cluttered reservoirs are reminders of the past months' times
so casually saved on dusty dresser tops with messy drawers,
in desks or within sturdy files on a closet shelf up high
which document the stories of our struggling financial lives
during the calendar year, now passed by and gone.

These tattered wrinkled documents of our days gone by,
of harried business trips and worrisome visits with doctors,
leisurely restaurant meals discussing business over food and drink,
and occasions of no tax consequence, reminders of fun to now discard;
as with skilled bookkeepers' diligence we will figure and sum
to find numbers now "deductible" in this year's legalese of IRS codes,
and add numerical columns as if these were the totals of our spent days.

In these winter months of tedious nervous paperwork,
some things have to do with our repulsion at government's greed
when we are compelled by cold and storm to stay indoors;
we'll do this revolting work in coffee-cup-mornings eaten away,
or spend late evenings wasted with office doors closed in solitude--
feeding quantification into computers or tiny boxes on printed paper,
as if this tax form representation really tells how our family life went.

We'll be given confidence soon by our hired preparation staff
in accounting firms and legal jargon interpretation offices
which do our expensive final processing until it's all formalized and done;
so when the paperwork is mailed away with our stifled grumbling complaints
and until payment checks are written out or electronic transfers made
so these have cleared our banking system and all assigned debt is paid;
for others and myself, Springtime begins when all annual tax work is done.

James R. Ellerston
January 18, 2023

It's Pretty

It's beautiful outside--
hoarfrost covering all the trees and power lines today,
as cold temperatures froze last night's fog
into a real winter wonderland;
in the morning pure, clean, an inch thick,
it was still clinging to the north side of the evergreens.

The sun warmed the temperatures today--
enough to cause the heavy coating on the trees to let go
with the resulting sound of small explosions, as the ice fell
from on high, to the ground under the tall cottonwoods;
the sound of the heavy ice dropping from bending boughs
sounding like music.

The farm acreage was so pretty yesterday evening--
as the sun set behind the tall old cedar trees,
reflecting off glaze-coated streets and flat fields;
some find their paradise in rural Iowa
on a day of frosted landscapes, bright sunshine, dark shadows,
a clear blue sky, and sunlight on white coated trees with no breeze.

While it's very nice to look at, and to take pictures of the snow and ice--
however, in wind gusts its weight is hard on trees and power lines;
later that day a sunset lined-up and shone down the small town's street;
the big moon was coming up in a clear blue eastern sky
while orange light silhouetted the outline of the large grain elevator;
lights illuminated a picnic shelter in a city park in the evening twilight.

James R. Ellerston
January 21, 2023
Facebook posts and photos by Glenn Henriksen Jan. 8, 9, 2023
Comments by Sue Wilson, Shirley Ohrtman, January 8, 2023
Comments by Charly Hertel, LaVonne Tow, Linda Thompson, Jan. 9, 2023

A Place You've Once Been

How do you feel when seeing it on television or in a film--
a place you've once been on your long-ago tourist travels,
on streets you've strolled and casually window-shopped,
and those historic buildings once entered in eager curiosity--
in fabled cities explored across the map and ever-smaller globe.

Does it not fill you with remorseful regret deep inside
to see what were once nearby sights that you rushed past on a hurried tour--
now realizing passing-up that optional side trip you chose to miss
was not a good choice for a day of vacation leisure,
and cost you memories that might have lasted a lifetime;
all skipped and squandered by saving a few ample coins--
and for a little lie-down time for minutes of an unneeded but desired nap.

The camera captured colors and hues on the final edited film--
maybe you just failed to see them at your sunset ride on a Venetian lagoon;
or river's curves missed on a distant horizon while gazing from a high tower;
there's a back table where we ate together in a darkened corner room--
that the movie replaced with a sidewalk cafe's bright daylit view.

Back then you had youth, good health, and fortune which let you travel;
memory's storehouse wasn't as aged and confused;
it is now so filled with times past, some good and some bad;
you once eagerly met new people, made new friends,
and bid farewells and painful goodbyes that were forever and sad;
now we see things in films' images close to our own past experiences--
like picture postcards a long-ago beloved has somehow sent to us.

James R. Ellerston
January 21, 2023

A Clouded-Over Monday Morning In January

I look outward at this gray January morning with a clouded brain;
Seeing out windows at haze causes me to turn inward from starting tasks,
have a hesitation to withdraw from post-holiday annual put-away jobs
and a new year of preparing tax records amid old boxed receipts--
to account for the busy transactions that had once been our busy life,
defining what we've survived and these cold days we now struggle through.

We now make plans for appointment dates on new bank picture calendars
they generously placed out for us in these winter months of the new year
but we must be so mindful of future weather's forecasts on nightly news
while our hearts look forward to the coming warmth of Spring sprouting hope
when outside activities can be done as planned and enjoyed in lighter dress
except hiking and campfire picnics outdoors in the park on rainy days.

We look forward to sailing waters with gentle winds to shape our sails
and lakeside friends to fill out summer teams and yacht-racing crews,
providing fulfilling companionship after our isolated homebound days;
while now we see squirrels scurry about on bare boughs and our yard fence
we look forward to hearing returning songbirds sing upon their leafy branches
as all creatures who flew south to escape the arctic blasts once again return.

James R. Ellerston
January 23, 2023

Massed Gun Violence

It is America's never ending plague with dozens of occurrences this year;
another two deadly outbreaks on a Monday in mid-January;
as cable-news reported the death of eleven in a coastal city
they had to cut away to the heartland-- to Des Moines, Iowa,
and report on attacks at a school leaving two dead and another injured;
there have repeatedly been mass shootings in just three weeks of this year.

Identifiable are several varieties of multiple shootings and killings,
which are taking place from coast to coast in different states and locals:
domestic conflicts, gang violence, random attacks by disturbed individuals,
attacks in stores and factories on co-workers, and terrorism, which often
stem from political, religious, social, racial, or of an environmental nature;
all of the incidents involve readily available highly effective killing tools.

Each mass shooting is an individual event involving different circumstances,
an incident with varied motivations and targeted victims--
all take place within a culture facilitating selling for profit deadly weapons--
making it easy for people with deadly intentions to acquire guns;
there are unimaginable losses suffered by victims and families; too often the
response has been to pray; some churches being reluctant to offer prayers.

James R. Ellerston
January 25, 2023
Adapted from "Gun Violence Is America's Never-Ending Plague"
by John Cassidy, The New Yorker online, January 24, 2023

Poems From My Daughter's Teenage Years

Me

I am not the social creature you see before you;
I am like a salamander
staying in the shade and the shadow,
hiding, staying out of sight if at all possible.

Quiet is my comfort food,
which I gnaw upon daily;
I am the sad, depressed, numb person inside my soul,
only revealed to the dark night and the cool earth.

Me, the one who lays around the house
staring at nothing with mind blank;
the one who watches the lightning
crack the clouds with its white light.

I'm laying on my carpet of green blades of grass
only me.

Julia K. Ellerston
Sometime in the 1996-97 school year
Edited James R. Ellerston December 4, 2023

After A Summer's Rain

Suspended droplets
hang from a limb of a tree
like stars hanging from strings in the sky;
these droplets capture the sunlight
of a summer's dream,
refracting it into a million colors
flashing out in brilliance
from the center of the crystalline tears
clinging to their branches.

Julia K. Ellerston
Sometime in the 1996-97 school year
Edited James R. Ellerston December 4, 2023

Night On The Lake

The lucid half moon shimmers
its silvery light upon the lake,
creating slivery waves
of sparkling, brilliant white
upon the waters of the lake;
the surf snakes along
to the wave-beaten sandy shore,
washing up sea shells;
the waves, with soft fingers,
carry the pale moonslivers
to crash them on the shore,
violently, in a crest of surf.

Julia K. Ellerston
Sometime in the 1996-97 school year
Edited James R. Ellerston December 4, 2023

Piano Sonata

Beautiful sixteenths
come down the keyboard;
heavy chords create
a basis for the flowing melody;
a minor gavotte
depicts an old dance;
the player continues
with a lively allegro;
both hands fly
in sixteenth note tempests,
and eighth notes
running up and down the keys;
the pianist finishes the song
with three chords,
hands floating to her lap;
she stands up and bows
amid thunderous applause.

Julia K. Ellerston
Sometime in the 1996-97 school year
Edited James R. Ellerston December 4, 2023

Looking To The Future

I can't look back now,
gotta face the present;
the eyes of the future are looking at me now--
deciding what will happen to me;
the past is like a fog,
shrouding around me.

But I face away from the morning mist
and look to the rising sun;
last night, I was prepared,
to leave behind my old teachers;
this morning, I am in Middle School,
not dear, old friendly elementary.

Julia K. Ellerston
Sometime in the 1996-97 school year
Edited James R. Ellerston December 4, 2023

Didn't Desire
A *Rumspringa*
But Searched
For A Pella
Of The Mind

Didn't Desire A *Rumspringa* But Searched For A Pella Of The Mind

I.

I grew up on a farm with other children of farm families
and we all knew what it was to work;
I went to school and church in an ethnically Danish Lutheran town
raised Presbyterian by ancestors of Scottish, Norwegian, and Quaker origin;
we had grown up hearing the Sonic Boom of SAC planes flying over farms
keeping A bombs airborne 24 hours daily during the 1961 Berlin Crisis
and 1963 Cuban Missile Crisis; the Nuclear Threat of radiation was so real;
at age eleven I had sandbagged the windows of our basement facing Omaha;
our Scout Troop went to school at night, learning to operate a geiger counter;
beer and liquor were always in a fridge, although smoking was discouraged;
Walter Conkrite was seated on the kitchen counter at supper time,
telling the honest news of the day and the body-count from Vietnam;
one meal my parents said it was OK if I went to Canada to avoid the War.

II.

In 1967 Central College hosted Dr. Martin Luther King a leader for civil rights,
who spoke peacefully to an audience gathered in a clay block gymnasium
after being escorted from a small airport down the highway,
when the capital city of Iowa didn't want to be securely involved that spring.

III.

In the summer of 1967 my mother attended a French language course,
and from Oakland University drove with some befriended nuns to hear,
and attended a piano recital in Detroit by the famous Van Cliburn
and in the summer darkness found herself driving home through an urban riot
saved from Black rioters she believed, when they pounded on their car,
because the Cadillac was filled with nuns dressed in their traditional habits.

IV.

Later that fall the nation saw the assassination of Dr. Martin Luther King--
who had spoken safely in Pella, Iowa-- and was now dead in Memphis, after
his dream of peacefully attaining Black freedom died on the memorial steps,
where Joan Baez had sung the song "Blowin' In The Wind", a classic,
written by a kid from Hibbing, Minnesota who had escaped the Iron Range
and a life in the mines to become the songwriter voice of my generation.

V.

In the middle of my high school senior year, I turned 18 on January 1, 1968
and signed up at the local Draft Board as required by Uncle Sam,
but the horrors of warfare were deferred for me as a student;
I continued studies and marched the graduation stage with a diploma in hand;
that spring of 1968 racial riots hit our nation's capital, and the slums burned
in Washington D.C., a smoldering city guarded by 11,000 government troops;
during the summer the bleeding head of Senator Robert F. Kennedy
was cradled in the hands of a 17 years old immigrant bus boy in a kitchen
of a California hotel before Kennedy later died of his wounds.

VI.

In my own idealized life I took off for a summer music camp at KU
and with 2200 high school students and spring graduates
walked the huge University of Kansas campus for six weeks of camp;
I lived in ten story dorms in innocence bliss, ignorant of external conflicts,
but leaving home made me feel more independent and confident inside.

VII.

In the fall of 1968 I became a college student, draft deferred,
and safely immersed in my Central College world, a mixture of diversity--
students from New York, New Jersey, and California interacting with Iowa;
in the dormitory if was a world of raw vocabulary and new ideas;
new lyrics and styles of rock music spun on vinyl played on record players
in poster splattered rooms scented with incense covered smoking habits.

VIII.

By spring guys' hair was unkempt and long, the daily uniform rugged,
the campus dress code was blue jeans, T-shirts and khaki;
inside myself, I searched and examined my own religious beliefs,
while outside the mainstream establishment a rhetoric emerged
that became anti-establishment, and anti military-industrial complex;
all this was kindled with the emerging anger at the War.

IX.

The summer of 1969 I returned home to the farm,
and six weeks of psychology class at the local community college,
and time with my family;
but the students from the East returned to campus newly energized--
some had actually been to the Woodstock Rock Festival,
an event that lifted music forever from its 45 r.p.m. world
and redefined the presentation of rock music and its important voice;
we didn't know much about it in rural Iowa;
Jimi Hendrix had given a defiant presentation of The Star Spangled Banner,
and his raw-edged distorted sound voiced a seething anger of young people
over the deaths in the Vietnam jungle.

X.

On December 1, 1969, our safe student-deferred-cocoon came to and end;
and the birthdates of young men were drawn from a lottery machine,
to determine the order in which they would be called-up
to die on the jungle floors by the establishment War machinery;
early December found us sitting under the sheltering snack bar's dome,
saying goodbye to those called-up for the War--that we'd never see again
when they went away at Christmas--never to graduate or return to classes--
and never recognized on those plastic plaques of graduates who served--
"after all they didn't graduate", (of course not, you idiots);
hopefully some made it across the Canadian border;
but I had won the only lottery I ever needed to win with number 305,
and I would never have to consider military service in my life again.

XI.

But as the war killing dragged on--
after all we must fight communism to bolster our Wall Street gambling,
and kill those Vietnamese babies in those wiped-out village pits;
at Central we wore armbands over our shirts to show our views--
those against the War, and those for the War;
political unrest grew in rhetoric at podiums on campuses across the nation,
and on May 4, 1970 in Kent, Ohio, the orders of a governor caused violence,
"eradicate the campus protestors" translated into a order to fire shouted out;
the Ohio National Guard stood on a knoll at Kent State University and shot
and murdered innocent college students, gunned down on their way to class;
the burst of firepower ignited riots and protests across the country;
white bed sheets with words in black paint floated against Central's buildings
in contrast with the stately brick of the campus in Pella, Iowa--
first on May 4 in the evening announcing the murders before evening meals
and May 5, calling for a student strike with no class attendance, mourning;
aware students marched that evening down Broadway to the city square,
for those few blocks escorted by the Pella Police to the commemoration,
where on the new Tulip Tower stage, a wise college president spoke words;
he did not distance himself, but took to the microphone with true eloquence,
(speaking words later quoted in church at his own memorial funeral service)
and my own sister strummed her guitar and sang out Bob Dylan's words
and the immortal "Blowin' In The Wind" echoed across the Pella downtown;
Central students returned to campus, studied, and finished out the term;
University of Iowa students were sent home and didn't complete the year;
the Math building was burned in Madison, the student union torched at KU;
it took 50 years until administration at Kent State participated with parents
of the deceased students to commemorate the killings on that campus;
Pella celebrated Tulip Time as usual; Central's band marched in parades;
What was the long life aftermath of all this unrest, protest, and violence,
which basically left our isolated and insulated life in Pella unscathed?

XII.

In my senior year at Central and planning afterward for graduate work,
for graduate school, I was admitted to the University of Kansas,
and accepted to be a counselor at Midwestern Music and Art Camp;
the job was important to me to help pay my way to summer school;
Sadly, I received in my last spring semester a notice that enrollment
at the summer camp had dropped-off so much that my employment
would not be needed-- due to the declining number of parents
willing to trust their students safety at a large university campus
that had displayed such violent student unrest;
(the camp is no longer a six week camp, but just one week).

XIII.

In my first job after graduation from Central I was employed in an Iowa city
that did not desegregate their schools until court ordered to do so in 1973;
while buying wedding china in 1978 I received a stern warning from a clerk
not to drive in certain parts of the city after dark;
I endured nearly forty years of teaching in that place during a long career,
teaching K-16, kindergarten through college seniors; some wonderful kids;
an arsonist burnt the century-old Lutheran church which was newly rebuilt;
a few years ago the pastor of that same church was murdered on the steps
of the church by a burglar hoping to rob him of an offering;
in January of 2023 while I visited friends they told me they had been warned
not to drive the street in front of a group of some apartment buildings
due to gunfire and gang violence there, this within a couple of blocks, where
the same street goes in front of the Catholic High School.

XIV.

Six years ago my wife and I moved from the city of our teaching careers,
raising our family in good schools, at church, and owned a first house;
we returned to live in Pella, where we had attended college after each other;
there we survived the first years of the Covid pandemic by staying home;
now the Ukrainian War invades our supper table with anger at the Russians;
Inside my own thoughts, I have always sought a place of refuge
and safety, a Pella, Iowa of the mind;
maybe it's the small town farm boy in me, still afraid of nuclear war;
(my new home has a windowless concrete room under the garage floor)
it really doesn't make me feel any safer in my eighth decade of life;
but I desire being home, and enjoying family,
while feeling reasonably safe and secure.

James R. Ellerston
January 26, 2023

Brisk Winter Days With Dark Nights

The Morning After That Night I Knew I'd Heard Talent

Natural talent bestowed has profited from past development,
producing a tone quality inspiring in its current sensitivity,
and well-chosen notes connected with electrifying precision,
with a sense of pitch matching unusually good;
your lines were imitative and unhindered in expression,
with flourishes complimenting and answering the singers,
inspired with creativity from inside-felt emotions;
your originality within the context of the chord progressions
gave people joy throughout the music shared with you.

You commanded your space and time with others on the stage
with an acoustic natural sound without enhancement,
and a graceful body moved in a subtle dance of muscled manhood;
popular music was inviting to a team of your youthful athletic friends--
these young people attended and cheered on another track team member,
and in proximity sat in auditorium rows close together;
within the hall we all floated airborne in your soaring sound,
profited from your experiences and current teaching
and your great love of the tenor sax as a musical instrument

Not until early the next morning, after my awakening at 5 a.m.,
was I flooded with a realization about what you were capable of doing--
that you do have a musical gift to offer to audiences;
talent was unveiled at the ALMA concert given last evening--
a performance inviting my return to this banquet of audible sounds,
to share another notable Friday night at an ALMA concert again;
I found a joy, not a mere evening of song and dance;
in the portrait of artistry unveiled and displayed upon a college stage,
all the songs were given freely from the students' hearts.

James R. Ellerston
February 11, 2021
Brian Hart played tenor sax at ALMA on February 10, 2023.
His friends from the Central College Track Team attended.

The Last Corn Shelling On That Farm

In dirt and dust and noise,
while working around the dangerous machines,
men in caps and bibbed overalls--
all these teen boys and rugged farmers of that day--
gathered in shared teamwork on that farm--
in the Iowa summer heat of July 1996.

They sweat moving their rakes, shovels, and tined forks--
removing the dry ear corn from the packed corn crib,
with its slatted wooden walls built by his own father in 1951,
a man who was still part of that day's working team;
he was driving the powerful green tractor which pulled heavy loads
of corn leveled to fill the sideboards to the top.

He pulled the large wagons on their big rubber tires
heaped heavily with bushels of yellow grain,
after the sheller had removed the kernels from the ears;
this Iowa farmer was still working at seventy-eight years of age
to haul the crop to town to market it
at the big concrete grain elevator in the town of Ringsted.

This once frequent farm life happening was captured on video
and seeing it replayed in 2023 was moving and poignant to view;
even the dryness of the pile of heaped brown cobs left behind,
or many workers gathered around a lunch table caught on camera;
these great memories were of a camaraderie amidst hard work,
of big farm dinners and lunch breaks that were looked forward to.

Today on the film we see a time that never will be repeated again
from a multi-generational family farm enterprise of a past era.
        James R. Ellerston   February 13, 2023
        Facebook post of Glenn Henriksen February 6, 2023
        Comment of Belva Ramler Henrickson

While On A Sunny Afternoon I Walked

Today open thawed pond water rippled in a breeze;
noisily the geese occupied rough tops of rocks and green mounds;
a few bravely returning fowl stood on brick-lined curving shores.

Among them some briskly fluttered their feathered wings,
and brashly honked-out their loud survival song
across an otherwise sleepy campus on this sunny afternoon.

James R. Ellerston
February 13, 2023

Just A Thought On A Monday

Not to build earthquake-proof housing and urban structures
is the big failure of architecture and housing design,
and is the cause of the number of victims
around the world in regions prone to quakes.

Great designer Frank Lloyd Wright built an earthquake-proof hotel
and it did survive the Japanese disaster in Tokyo in 1923
surviving until demolition at the hands of the unappreciative,
failing in its lessons of design and cost worthiness as value.

To not build in a safe way is a poor pattern for future safety--
such designs could be criminal and inhumane to a future life
on an unstable planet with shifting tectonic plates
and the horrors of death and injury falling buildings cause.

James R. Ellerston
February 13, 2023
A thought following the Turkish-Syrian earthquake of 2023.

The Wonders In Our Worlds Of Memory

It is by remembering that we define ourselves;
memory is a photograph or sensation in the mind of a time and location,
a scent remembered of a place or person dear, or the stench of warfare;
somewhere that can be currently traveled to today from a distance.

We may recall the sound of a voice that became beloved for tone and text,
imagine a past touch longed-for when in a lonely bed, feeling a chilling night,
with a patter of rain falling on the roof, without arm's sheltering us in a storm;
a painful death grieved as a recurring pain, repeatedly stabs us with grief.

There was warmth in a cattle-filled barn, with breath steaming the winter air;
melody or lyrics of a song may sound over and over, echoing in one's head,
transporting us back to be with just one single person, no one but a beloved;
we retain the physical pattern of movements at an occasion on a dance floor.

We once watched physical hand and arm patterns of a great violinist,
had keen inspirations in moments at a concert or insights at an art gallery;
we retain nursery rhymes, words of poetry, or dialog delivered on a stage;
we feel an ache in our heart forever, feeling absence for things gone from us.

Within consciousness and subconscious remembering, we are who we are,
memory is a fluid reservoir defining our choices, the things we choose to do;
our own previous experiences clarify our interpretations of others' actions
and how we see ourselves within our own creative and daily social lives;

Acts of generous goodness give us faith, and hope for the future of mankind;
we carry such acts forward, nurturing others as if our own blessed children,
feeling love for others from infancy to grave, until our own days' ending;
we must remember our own travels, so we never forget how to go home.

James R. Ellerston
February 16, 2023

Memories Of Watery Places Over Time

I was haunted last evening by a past memory
of a row of white lavatories I still see in my mind
in a men's shower room of a dormitory bathroom
that I had planned to use and quickly leave;
but my memory stored up the row of white sinks
from that day in Eisenstadt, Austria
thirty-five years earlier.

The sounds I heard there are gone now;
they had come from a grown man, a naval veteran
weeping again the torturous question
of why he had survived
while so many shipmates perished in the sea
when his ship had gone down in WWII,
so many years before.

That day, so many years ago, I heard him sob;
now, decades later I can still see the room
and a row of white sinks
in the clouded light of a long past day--
where he had stood crying out his grief
when I had hurriedly entered,
and overheard his decades of internal pain.

James R. Ellerston
March 12, 2023
Alex Bew and wife Betty Bew attended several International String
Workshops, and we became friends on the post-workshop tour
around Austria in 1988, a friendship that lasted until their deaths.

I have so many words

I have so many words for the same few ideas.
A lexicon of redundant synonyms and frivolous
adjectives creating an illusion of depth.
But this circle is not a sphere

I have many words for few ideas.
A lexicon of synonyms and antonyms
That give an illusion of depth
But this circle is not a sphere

Many words, few ideas
Synonyms, adjectives--
An illusion of depth
Circle, not Sphere

Stefan Crowl
February 21, 2023

Last Look Around A House Of Past Memories

Old locks turned with keys and a door opened into history;
a storm door tapped the heels of a parade of athletic shoes;
light streamed through large oak-trimmed windows
where white sheer-style curtains diffused bright daylight.

Young men's excited exclamations echoed in the bare rooms
on this final visit of grandsons to their grandparent's house
before the "For Sale" sign would be staked outside in the yard,
with a finality to a place where parents had raised their children.

For some, silent voices from the past still live within these walls,
from when generations had gathered around a supper table,
where today a father had brought his three boys to see once again
what remained of their family's history now past.

The son's antics attempted to bring humor to a somber occasion;
cardboard boxes sat in the corner of the emptied basement room,
holding few reminders of previous living in a now vacant structure,
this place all members in a family once called "home".

The residence was on what had once been their familiar street,
in an area once thought of as "our" neighborhood,
in a community thought of as a "hometown",
where children once born were raised in a close unit there.

James R. Ellerston
March 3, 2023
Facebook post and photos of Bret Crowl on March 2, 2023
Bret Crowl showed his sons Ryan, Stefan, and Ian the house of the
boy's grandparents, Grandpa Phil and Grandma Wilm, in
Humboldt, Iowa.

Spring Flowers Grew And Ideas Bloomed

The Flag Was Pulled Down And I Questioned Our Lives

As I walked about my chosen paths today
on a silver shaft I viewed a half-masted flag
across the way in its windy flight drawn half-way low
so as not to freely sail its course but strongly anchored stay
on this windy Tuesday afternoon of our harried lives--
as if it was a vessel tethered to the pier at voyages end,
like blossoming lives of children cut short by untimely deaths.

Their student days ended with more bullets firing hatred again,
in yet another school room violated in our violent land--
the repeated teaching of a hard lesson of contemporary life--
that a weapon of war or inciteful words in the wrong hands,
could silence a future poet, who in their own free expression,
might fly straight out from a common pole of truth and wave bravely
on a day of reddened-face falsehood capped in blue causing harm.

Don't be that weak beating heart who would not really teach,
nor one who fails to print what is really going round,
all those tragic things in news reports today coming down--
because of a frightening failure to sense real history being made--
those just breathing a false patriotism of the right to a smoking gun,
but deny reading as if the nation's banner was blowing straight aloft
at the top of a pole, in display of human pride and loving goodness.

James R. Ellerston
March 29, 2023
On March 27, 2023, 3 students and 3 staff were killed in a classroom in The Covenant School in the Green Hills neighborhood of Nashville, Tennessee. The suspected shooter was also killed.

On A Walk Together

On a sunny afternoon walk around familiar places
a glint of reflected sunshine caught an observant eye
and he bent his flexible back and reached-out for it,
kneeling down on one knee on the walkway.

His fingers coached jagged glass in fragile broken brownness
into his outstretched hand from the blackness of tilled garden dirt
amid shrubs in a tended bed before the college dormitory,
where the carelessly thrown bottle had shattered when planted.

In youthful days, while trodding a campus yet new to him,
he knew what to do out of respect for Earth and others--
concern for future gardners' fingers working moistened soil,
cared that summer school students' bare feet might step there.

So in afternoon heat he knelt and picked up the muddy shards--
still with their torn paper label attached with glue;
he deposited the glass in a nearby refuse bin along the alley;
it was his small effort on that day for a better world.

James R. Ellerston
April 1-2, 2023
Ezra Blasi is a student at Central College in Pella, Iowa

With Grandpa's Microscope

It is morning by the window
light focused by lenses
curiosity,
concentration
using vision
an eye on the tiny unseen
a world obscured by minimal size
yet all around us.

A grandson on a chair
peering into the metal tube
ground glass opening a view
while at a table with his grandpa
a four year old attempts
to see the wonderment
on a slide of an object
caught between two sheets of glass.

These moments opening up a horizon
of possibilities and awareness
imagination
with a Christmas gift to Grandpa when he was eight
almost sixty-five years ago
a tiny world seen and shared
in a few brief hours today;
have you see it?

James R. Ellerston
April 1, 2023
With Grandson Liam and Bryce on March 31, 2023

Around The Campus

Only the day before I'd seen the two of them
sitting and swinging on the seat by the water,
their four shoes moving in unison, heel and toe,
creating the back and forth motion of the hanging seat
with its chain links suspended in the endless time
of a couple's love on a sunny afternoon.

Today a solitary girl sat there alone by herself,
but the swing moved back and forth in rhythm
set in motion by her flexing feet--
the bench giving support in the heated air;
in my ignorance, I mistook her for an earlier day's memory
and inquired about where her boyfriend was today.

She replied calmly, like geese moving on the pond and island,
"He's in Ireland, on study abroad";
my curiosity asked, "What city and how long?"
"He's in Belfast for a semester in Northern Ireland,
they just celebrated an anniversary of the Good Friday Truce";
I talked about "Derry Girls", its humor and pathos on my Netflix screen.

It's such an interesting comedy about religious tragedy and conflict,
the impact of border controls, passports, and building walls between people;
Our brief conversation came to an end, and I walked away;
I continued with my afternoon exercising about the campus,
but that time we chatted will give her an understanding, if she views the comedy,
which will show what her guy experienced first hand across the ocean.

James R. Ellerston
April 14, 2023

In 1998 a truce known as the Good Friday Agreement, created an end to The Troubles in Northern Ireland. U.S. President Joe Biden went to Ireland for the 25th Anniversary of the agreement, for a four day visit, in April of 2023. He was the fourth U.S. President to visit Ireland, after JFK, Ronald Reagan, and Bill Clinton.

Given Yet Another Chance For My Heart To Go On

In a somber tone it was announced that 111 years ago on this very day
the majestic new steaming ship had met its untimely watery grave--
but as a sea of crisp dollar bills waived in the air above the cheering crowd,
and fluttered in clouds descending to the floor-- to be retrieved for charity,
audience generosity did not let isolated endangered hearts go on alone.

An evening never dragged in form-defining costumes, highlighting makeup,
and utilizing skillful dance movements, mime, and lip-synced songs,
until suddenly a brief popular song reminded us that a single block of ice
looming ahead could condemn unfortunate souls to the ocean depths
many years too early in their lifespan, on their own dark and foggy night.

Here in this Central community of united charitable hearts,
when love circled around a hall in celebration with many cell phones waving
--with differences accepted and outreached hands to offer support,
an effort was made tonight to provide lifeboats to persons across the state
needing encouragement while adrift in a hateful world.

We might avoid a cold collision with older frozen social values
if our hearts open up, we can free our outlook, vision, and tunneled viewpoint
with an alteration to our society's vengeful, arrogant course;
we would see dangers in our direction and callous speed of decision-making,
and change our chosen rate of over-reaction, in time to make a difference.

On our life's busy travels we were given this star-struck brilliant evening,
when all together celebrated the dancing on the runway and about the floor;
we all can't finish every voyage, or share a floating door on troubled seas;
but if we seriously accept personal differences, if others' lives are affirmed,
if we could share unbounded offers of our love, more will choose to live on.

James R. Ellerston
April 16, 2023
The Central College student organization Common Ground presented their
annual fundraising Drag Show on Saturday April 15, 2023 starting at 9 p.m.
as a fundraiser for the campus organization and people around Iowa.

He Spoke At The Tulip Tower May 8, 1970

During the course of the last week
I have been haunted by a line from a poem
which I have not thought of for many years.
I don't recall the author or the title
but the words and mood they invoke are clear.

The poem describes two people and a wooded landscape.
All seems natural and beautiful but the last line of several stanzas ends
with the words "and no birds sing". There is a feeling of incompleteness,
a sense of desolation and a nightmarish quality
which makes everything normal and happy appear sinister and incomplete.

It is a feeling appropriate for our times! "and no birds sing."
We work and play, study and strike,
we enjoy the gaiety of a tulip time or a rock concert,
but beneath it all there is a feeling that things have come unhinged,
a sense that our world is unreal and irrational.

People seem to feel caught up in tragic events over which they have no control.
Young lives of students are lost-- snuffed out in acts without reason
on campuses where reason supposedly reaches its highest development.
Young soldiers in the prime of live are lost forever
as human testimony of man's inability to live at peace with his fellow man.

Violence erupts in the pursuit of non-violence.
The pursuit of peace finds fulfillment in war.
The search for love breeds hate and alienation.
We sing our songs and do our things--
but "no birds sing."

But in the depths of our despair there is a glimmer of light in the darkness.
The sorrow and agony over the loss of young lives can produce
the deep impact necessary to begin to change lives.
And that is where it all begins. Not in the pursuit of great causes,
but in the building of genuine relationships with each other.

Lives must be changed.
In some cases this is a simplistic conversion experience
summarized as "finding Christ." In others it is a complex interrelationship
of events, experiences, relationships with people and meditation.
But the result is a denial of self and a concern for others.

From this comes community and joint causes. Commitment and concern.
Caring and completeness. If the deaths of young people can really move us--
begin a change in us as individuals, and unite us in our concerns:
we will begin to transform alienation into understanding,
exploitation into assistance; war into peace!

We will sing our songs and "do our things,"
and the birds will sing again.

Address by Dr. Ken Weller, President of Central College, as part of the Central College March for Peace. Delivered at the Tulip Tower in the town square of Pella, Iowa May 8, 1970 after the deaths at Kent State University in Ohio on May 4, 1970 earlier. Poem title by John Keats, "La Belle Dame Sans Merci".
The address was again read out at Dr. Weller's memorial service at 2nd Reformed Church in Pella during April 2022. Typescript provided by the Weller family to James R. Ellerston in March 2023, who set the words in this form.

Written For Widowers, Everyone

Over the many grieving years
their heart could not have grown any fonder--
for beautiful love does not wane or wax with passion,
nor its bright light dim with the passage of seasons;
one's anguish does not lesson in phases with stretches of time
after the tragic human reality of death.

Absence stares back each morning when they awaken--
with the unused pillow in the space next to their's,
an empty chair and place across the breakfast table,
left-overs thrown out of the fridge which would have fed the other,
the continuous babble of broadcast media playing incessantly
to loudly drown out the unrelenting silence of an absent laughter.

They miss a beloved's voice speaking love in casual phrases,
and miss the shuffle of slippers over the floors of a busy home;
they long for the ecstasy of touch and sheltering hugging arms;
it's tough to get through every calendar day by oneself alone;
some decorate a cozy space and collect art,
and others just hoard things reminding them of a past life period.

No effort at artistic interior design can take away the broken heart,
or phase out the long term grief of the survivor,
when the one true love of a brief earthly life
is the first to pass away, leaving the other person living on alone,
to experience years of bright sunrises, dwelling without a partner
in a room, where the greener grass keeps on growing outside.

James R. Ellerston
May 22, 2023
Written for a friend at the fifteenth anniversary of his wife's death.

Boston In Springtime

Boston In The Spring (May 9-14, 2023)

I.

Our weather was always sunny, air fresh and pleasant,
a tidal sea undulated under the hull;
the Mayflower II moved against its dock lines;
my seven-years-old grandson eagerly strode the decks
and saw the stern-aiming cannons for warding off pirates;
time spent with his mother, my daughter, on a trip to Boston;
but this day we were on the coast at Plymouth
where we saw the famous stone
under an enshrining Greek-styled temple of protection
where today we were the sightseeing pilgrims,
transported down the busy Cape highway by car
on a Friday morning by a skilled and able driver
to tour one of three ships we stepped aboard
while on this trip to Massachusetts in the Spring.

II.

A chair-filled stage was well lit, yet the grand ballroom was dim
for the impressive graduation ceremony,
where my daughter had walked
across a platform with dignitaries and faculty
in the vastness of the Boston Convention Center,
wearing her newly acquired hat, robe, and academic regalia--
her robe's sleeves now with the three black velvet stripes,
and wearing a colored doctoral hood in the colors of the institution--
celebrating studying for a Clinical Doctorate Degree,
the first cohort of classmates in this program from the
Institute of Health Professionals
of Massachusetts General Hospital.

III.

As our five days in the Boston area went on,
we learned how convenient our hotel location was;
our family walked to her cohort's graduation reception
and presentation of posters describing clinical research
at a building part of Massachusetts General Hospital
just outside the gate of the Charleston Navy Yard,
with views of docked pleasure boats and morning harbor sailors
seen from its terrace, while standing outside in the breeze;
our daughter had proudly stood before the gathered group
attentively gazing at the throat-scoped photos of vocal folds
amid descriptors of pathological problems for the pictures.

IV.

People must have been shorter back then in 1812;
as I toured three decks of the actual original sailing frigate,
a vessel known as the US Constitution or "Old Ironsides",
utilizing the rope-railed ship's stairs to descend two decks below,
I moved about beneath low beams and saw sailors' hammocks,
and moved past cannons aimed from the side portals;
I saw a glimpse of officers' quarters in the stern
and wooden masts and rigging towering overhead.

V.

The Navy base had the USS Cassin Young staffed by volunteers,
a steel hulled Fletcher class destroyer, it had survived WWII;
we walked a main deck with open portals to Navy shipboard lives;
mess, dining, radio room were all open to see within
from starboard or port sides of the large vessel tied up dockside;
one did not feel movements of the hull beneath us;
this due to the time of day relative to the tides or its sheer size.

VI.

The Warren Tavern in Charleston was blocks from our hotel
in an area of residences and retail shopping;
the 1780 tavern had existed here in early American historic times,
and George Washington and Paul Revere had been patrons;
we dined twice beneath the low dark-beamed ceiling,
eating traditional restaurant foods and drink,
seated at a table near multi-paned windows;
a colonial building, it now had a tiny men's room,
a fireplace and an outdoor dining terrace;
there is a local fable about a bench carving but this was myth--
there was no furniture dating to revolutionary times
with the initials of George Washington in it.

VII.

A late afternoon trip was made to see a sculpture based on a book-
a row of ducks, Mrs. Mallard, and eight ducklings in a city park;
individual sculptures for each named duckling, eight of them--
Jack, Kack, Lack, Mack, Nack, Oack, Pack, and Quack;
the book was Make Way For Ducklings by Robert McCloskey,
winner of The Caldecott Medal for children's literature in 1941;
the bronzes in the park had a golden shine,
polished when children climbed and sat on them,
as my grandson had ridden the "mother" statue
while we snapped photos in spring Massachusetts weather,
on a sunny afternoon in a populated park space in Boston.

VIII.

We experienced six tourist days of sunny weather and good food,
with views dominated by the skyline of downtown Boston buildings,
and two great cable-strung towers of the Leonard P. Zakim Bridge
with traveling traffic racing past, except when in an agonizing crawl.

IX.

Our connecting flight home was through a New York City airport,
and as the plane banked over the harbor and rivers,
our port side window allowed aerial views of the great bridges,
the shrines of democracy in the harbor--
the Statue of Liberty and Ellis Island;
the great stone arches of the Brooklyn Bridge
crossing the East River were not too distant;
we saw the iconic skyscrapers of Manhattan Island
before our touch down on the LaGuardia runway
and the twenty-five minute walk to our departure gate 70.

X.

After our longer second flight we were soon home again in Iowa,
driven by our son and friend from Des Moines to the city of Pella,
we live in winters where my wife and I spent our college years,
having good times together amongst the tulips and flower gardens
as the sun rises and sets each day in our retired lives.

James R. Ellerston
May 16, 2023
Thank You:
To our five day driver, Richard for his safety and expert guidance.
To a Portland, Oregon student watching my safety on Constitution.
To my wife's hometown friend who met us for dinner our last night.
To my daughter prompting a trip to celebrate her accomplishment.
To our grandson who gave us so much love and pleasure.
To the Boston college student who showed us the medical store.
To all who put out their arms to steady me on steps and slopes.
To Max who drove to the DSM airport and returned our car home.
To my son and friend who waited at DSM to drive us home to Pella.

Wisconsin Cabin Opened-Up Lives

For A Dear Young Friend

Each night when I pop my Tombstone pizza in to cook,
after removing it from a wrapped stack in my freezer,
and having effortlessly pre-heated an electric oven in my home--
I'll think of the true cost of my food to him, and others,
standing on the night shift in the Nestle´ plant in Medford.

He works five nights a week for nearly twelve hours,
getting a couple of breaks and eating a sack-lunch meal
earning the money to support a young life--
paying rent on an apartment where he lives with his gal,
napping through daylight hours in short spurts of sleep.

I've witnessed a young man's struggle for wakeful alertness,
for doing the once most mundane tasks for his mechanic's mind,
seeing him repairing my lawn mower with his girl as a team--
and watched while he dozed in comfortable bliss on my couch,
with a head cradled in a lap in trusting love.

Yes, my pizza tastes really fine, as always,
still made by caring people in a Wisconsin town, as always,
shipped around the nation by a big fleet of trucks, as always--
generating steady employment for people for decades, as always,
helping fund a local economy that prospers, as always.

Pizza-making built a community center for ice skating and hockey
where my own children learned to skate when at Grandpa's house;
and it now provides a job for someone I personally know and love--
there is just a chance that the supper my wife and I will eat together
had moved down the line in front of you, my friend, at night.

James R. Ellerston
June 9, 2022
For Nick Ludwig

After Another Year: A 2023 Trip To See My Wisconsin Friends

I.

I know they live in a world of long hours and repetitive work;
often around noisy machines,
they have a knowledgeable respect for old vehicles
and engines needing overhauls;
miles could be walked in their steel-toed shoes
or worn boots of manure-covered cracked leather

After another winter had passed I encountered my young people
having not only an actual hunger for food,
but starved for someone to listen to them
and try to understand their individual lives,
and they talked with another person they could trust
about their inner feelings and details of past days.

II.

I had followed a red pickup that afternoon
so visit the goat farm of another friend's family,
curious to see the animals that had prompted a Facebook picture.

I stood on a green grass lawn beside the gravel drive,
and people had come out from the farmhouse
while the animals bleated from their pen and ducks waddled about.

I was embarrassed that I had not recognized two of them
after the rapid maturing transformation into young manhood,
an overtaking of the once teenaged bodies with dramatic changes.

I was surprised by the red beard on a boy I remembered as blond,
but the hair bristled there in manly glory on his chin and neck,
below welcoming eyes that hid the deepness of his thoughts.

I had forgotten how short in stature, compared to me, that one was,
and while the guy had matured in face and manner,
when introducing himself, his voice sounded its familiar resonance.

I saw him hold goats tenderly within strong encircling arms,
and the animals making affectionate licks upon his face
after he guided them out of the barn into the sunlit pen.

I met a father who climbed off from his lawn tractor mower,
pausing to meet this gray-haired man from Iowa,
and I chatted with the mother of this now long-haired son.

III.

I drove miles of challenging dusty country gravel roads--
guided and directed on the route to a dairy operation,
and two toured me past lots of Holstein cows
and they greeted some by name or by ear tag number.

Together we walked through the barns where they daily worked,
opening and closing gates as I saw parts of a real working farm,
where they drove tractors through the fields
and cared for the animals within these mammoth sheds.

IV.

We traveled next to our own lakeside home-- where a smokey fire
made a futile attempt at suppressing hordes of mosquitoes;
our annual picnic supper offered up wieners and brats in buns.

I heard comments and stories from all of them in the group--
but only words of longing for Arizona from the new girl of one,
while guys revealed their anguished past from childhood 'til now.

I heard with open appreciative ears of their past pains--
and affirmation of my own part in their lives-- providing opportunities
for work, earnings, friendship, and gifts arriving at timely moments.

I admire their work ethic, ambition, and willingness to tackle tasks;
and show concern for strangers, friends, and family;
they can repair machines and farm the land; they respect nature.

I've made no efforts and done few things transforming their lives,
but want them to always know, never in long years ahead forget,
that this poet loved them; they are worthy of being loved by others.

V.

Once more now, at age 73, I am at the family house in Wisconsin
gazing out from a row of windows at reflections on peaceful waters,
seeing blue sky and green trees in sunlit splendor;
all fill my morning vision with a joy at life and being here.

I have safely traveled the distance for nine daylight hours,
on expressways and tight curves through country spaces,
by wooded river bluffs and rural farmers' fields;
it was a full day of attentive effort at guiding my car to get here.

The trip filled my hours with frequent braking and shifting gears,
as I climbed my way northward and eastward on the road maps,
driving more direct highways within three states to reach that place,
a small lake we have called "Thomat" through the decades.

"Thomat" is a contraction of two 1948 owners' names,
where the families we know have ventured since--
a heritage always passed down-- to now four younger generations;
one more I have made my early warm weather sojourn here.

In Spring and Fall I pilgrimage here to see a natural forested land,
and visit my young friends, who have survived another winter;
their smiles fill me with a happiness that I have come to love;
and this year again we shared good times together on a weekend.

VI. Thoughtlessly Distanced

When a real distance develops between people
it's not hundreds of miles that separate them,
or the nine hours of driving time that one must come,
nor a lack of frequent visiting minutes face to face,
not a mere passage of time or the passing of seasons creating space;
long-term friends can meet again, as if still in yesterday;
for in any relationship one shouldn't ever let a stranger develop--
distanced by a silly fight over a caring concern,
or too many empty places across a table at different meal times.

One might have been tempted to misrepresent to the other by telling falsehoods,
not disclosing true intentions nor been honest about travel destinations
or have violated loyal honesty in a living partnership gone wrong,
as another shared their physical space while another toiled at a job;
by one ingesting mind-altering substances for an escape elsewhere,
no longer honoring or caring for possessions given as gifts in friendship;
but maybe simply selling home contents supporting their drug habit,
or attacked a friend as a scapegoat in defense when emotionally upset;
it is always wrong to blame a person reaching out trying to understand another.

Great gaps can be overcome by open communication in times of need,
sometimes learning to ask for real advice when frightened by worry,
making efforts at real empathy with another's way of expressing their distress,
avoiding using an acquaintance as a target in anger at one's own shortcomings;
utilize the computer in the palm of one's hand to tell what's needed;
learn to speak respectfully to others experiencing mutual personal pain;
don't throw up a wall against a person who only tried to help a friend,
while all had made their best efforts, with their limited knowledge in the moment;
we must try to understand what to really do for a person in a true friendship.

VII. So Briefly In An Open-Armed Hug

There are so few moments of true understanding
in our world of rapidly changing lives and situations--
while existing in our fragile flesh and bodies, minds and thoughts;
we have too few times for real communication with others.

We're not speaking of voicing just daily mundane needs
or blandly repeating the news commentators' opinions--
but bravely talking about our previous experiences and feelings,
expressing joys, honest pain, and raging anger openly into a room.

What we say needs hearing by open-minded persons or friends,
someone who hopefully will understand where we come from--
why we are the way we are or before once were,
however long or briefly in each phase or stage we lived.

All must realize it was difficult for each person, being their own "me"
throughout days and years of changes, in youth, maturity, aging,
we need to know another will not alter their good opinion of us--
but after telling of struggles, continue to offer real love, all our days.

VIII. Homeward Bound

This day for leaving Wisconsin the car was packed by midmorning;
it was to be a long drive home ahead,
but time was taken to deliver lunch to two friends,
ambitious young guys working on a dairy farm--
they live days of cows and tractors;
in a farmyard they gobbled down cold pizza baked earlier that day,
actually purchased by one of them for my evening supper,
finally pulled from the freezer for this old man's breakfast,
long before his two missed highway turns added extra miles.

That afternoon distances were driven in wrong directions twice,
and backtracked after a realization of those errors had occurred;
and on a route home again stretched into the sunset
and into encroaching darkness as swiftly hours passed
on two lane roads through Iowa farmland,
with the blinding glare of oncoming car lights;
this reactive old person's nerves were braking hard at each--
my car crouched instinctively near the right shoulder at each pass;
but I survived and reached home exhausted, later than expected.

James R. Ellerston
May 27, 29, 30, 31, June 2, 2023
For Nick Avery Ludwig, Austin Olson, and Brok Hathaway,
 in and near Medford, Wisconsin
"Thomat" is a lake of 5.2 acres in Taylor County, Wisconsin
reached after travels through eastern Iowa, south-eastern
Minnesota, and south-western Wisconsin

At A Minnesota Lake
For A Summer Of Fun

Smoke Again in 2023

Smokiness smothers my soaring summer dreams
as wildfires roar far away to the north again;
our shoreline views are obstructed;
oh how silently I see smoke sailing my inland sea.

Smoke tints sun's voyage a colored haze,
causing smelling, sniffing, sneezing,
stuffiness makes my sinuses enraged;
struggling for breath stifles daily ambitions.

Moving southward a sleepless blanket snuggles my vacation;
a smugglers stinky shroud covers my lake,
hiding a true vision of the beauty in rural areas,
with shadows obscuring a sharpness of focus.

Familiar scenery is confused by the blurry fogginess,
while hazardous particles make us worried;
hidden normal clarity is still present in cloudy obscurity;
it's a truly hideous deception of the normal reality at this lake.

The smoke is a hider of the natural beauty--
this haziness which has moved in across international borders,
and which is a disguiser of a normal sunny day--
windblown for such far distances around the planet.

Current conditions are a pariah for asthmatics,
and are an ongoing plague for air quality watch dogs;
is it an alarm to alert us to take action
while with the moving clouds we await the acid rain?

James R. Ellerston
June 17, 2023

Not Really Out Of The Woods Yet

Managing loneliness is a difficult part of life;
when we are in situations separate and alone,
while in familiar localities of time and place,
or settings once in the past familiar
that may now feel like we're in a new environment.

I go a long distance to the forest and lakeside cabin
to commune with nature in a setting of beauty,
escaping social demands of weekly schedules,
and missing my companions at home and afar--
but not enjoying daily idea-sharing with persons I call friends.

We people are social beings and desire companionship;
our human bodies desire the feel of hugs and muscles holding us;
we want to hear sounds of soothing loving voices and gentle words;
our beings long for the confirmation of parental roles;
seeking physical contact, and the touch of others.

Now mature, I yearn for meaningful conversations,
interchanging ideas and divergent viewpoints,
with another who will listen to my thoughts and concerns,
someone participating in dialogue about feelings--
where together words and actions make a difference in our days.

James R. Ellerston
June 19, 2023

Today

Today in our morning sunshine
    the distant trees look green;
white capped waves are rolling in
    with foam upon my beach of sloping sand;
whistling wind blows from out of the southeast land--
    so I'm breathing freely these early hours;
the moving air is clean and fresh
    no smoke is in our vision or near at hand;
we see blue cloudless skies and moving water
    and breathe air that's clear and clean;
I'm hoping for a better day
    than those in our previous gray cloudy week;
but the view is here to savor and enjoy through windows' glass
    with each and every look encouraging an outward peak;
hopefully warmer weather is here to stay,
    and smoke-free days a while will last.

James R. Ellerston
June 20, 2023

Bryce's 8th Birthday

This is a day for you that's great;
it is your yearly birthday when today you've turned eight;
more months have added up in totaled years,
and now older and wiser you have daily grown
in appetite and strength of back and limb,
with new height of stature and shapely boyish form.

You've acquired new skills practicing daily,
and have growing wisdom and understanding;
you can somehow ask more mature questions,
and will give replies with somewhat intelligible answers;
you have gained a lot in musicianship
and skill playing musically on your violin.

Here I'm hoping you keep a positive viewpoint--
enjoying other family members, and the activities you do;
look for the best in other people, find something good to like;
there is beauty all around us, try to see it;
all will eventually turn out just fine,
and on June 20 in 2024 you will be nine.

James R. Ellerston
June 20, 2023

With A Hot Coffee Prelude

In early morning hours of each day
with coffee cup in hand,
we sit and often hear the waves come in
ending their rolling travels on the beach;
it is for me a welcome crashing sound they make--
while easing me awake and active.

My breakfast biscuit is squeezed between my fingers,
each crisp bite a welcome taste;
some is broken-off and shared with my pooch
as he lays in welcomed "good dog" comfort at my feet;
it is a sunrise ritual to sip, brew, and eat--
in almost silent solitude within our chairs.

We shelter inside a lakeside sturdily built cabin
which has stood the test of many decades' time
on my family's cherished sandy shore;
so today we'll share another cuppa together
in daybreak hours while fog rolls off--
and golden sunlit times briefly fill shared lives.

James R. Ellerston
June 21, 2023

Summer Solstice

The longest day of summer has gone past
while Earth tilted in rotation on its planetary voyage,
and though mankind's clocks still kept their even numbered hours,
daily amounts of bright daylight and dimmed nighttime vary.

Through our long twelve month trip around our sun,
except for calculated miniscule seconds all in accumulation
so every fourth year during February sees an added entire day
in a leap year darker second month of 29 longer winter nights.

In this third week of calendar's sixth month of June
we came to a numerical 21 within its little square,
but we made no special activities or druidic celebrations
and ran our errands, went our ways, did chores around our homes.

More minutes were added of evening light but passed unnoticed;
our latitude isn't far enough north to experience "white nights",
and we went between our bed sheets early on the clock,
scarcely having changed routines except for the heat of summer.

James R. Ellerston
June 22, 2023

Morning Meditation

Today the sky is an even cloudy gray;
it's quiet since no waves lap my north shore beach;
the gentle breeze alas is from the north
and more smoke will drift our way;
from flaming distant forests comes the silent haze,
a constant irritant to stinging eye and coughing lung,
spread widely over states and great cities far flung.

One wishes for clear blue heavens floating above
and golden sunshine rays tanning my winter-paled skin;
yesterday visiting company started their many miles toward home--
one cabin has empty rooms, and piled sheets to wash and dry;
in the long bright evenings of these late June weeks,
we finally saw a colorful sunset above west shoreline trees
before six long hours of darkness did again begin.

I was sleeping several blessed hours solid in a row
between our dog's trips out into the backyard to go;
and my own nocturnal toilet usage in early morning hours--
bladder reminders in a night spent in breath-assisted slumbering,
before a window is again guarded by sitting in a comfortable chair,
peering outside through a mosquito pattern on a blocking screen
watching the peaceful day unfold in placid silence.

James R. Ellerston
June 23, 2023

Turtle Town Art Fair

I heard rain softly patter on the roof
sounding like a soft *pianissimo* roll in an orchestral score;
without a pattern drops dimpled the silver surface of the lake;
a bird hopped on dock and sand; a chipmunk scurried about.

I bit a piece from a banana, the first part of my breakfast;
hot coffee brewed noisily in a clear glass pot;
yogurt and its spoon stood at attention for later dining;
peanut and almond bars were in formation on my tabletop.

With wrapper peeled, notes of chocolate tantalized my tongue,
and I sipped warm liquid from a red ceramic mug;
looking out at swirling patterns from air moving the water's surface,
I hoped morning showers stopped for a trip to a small town art fair.

I did not contemplate making any huge cash purchases today,
but didn't know what sudden impulse to buy might chance occur--
so my wife and I traveled familiar scenic roads through forests
to wander a church yard and parking lot to maybe buy a treasure.

James R. Ellerston
June 24, 2023

Another Saturday July 1st

At first light a chorus of songbirds chirped together,
their combined melodies were singing through my open window
as cool moving air wafted across my bare well-rested skin,
and a percussive woodpecker tapped-out his cadence on a tree;
a crow called out from a distant yard down the street,
while a lone fisherman glided in isolated search, in his drifting boat
upon the silent wakeless surface of the morning lake,
on this holiday weekend just coming alive today.

Friday, on the day before, the noisy lawn machines worked hours;
weed-eaters and mowers roared their paths across fields of grass;
leaf blowers cleared sidewalks and driveways; vacuums moaned;
noisy chainsaws tore away at restful quiet hours felling trees,
those now seen as grown to close to cabins in maturity,
engines rasped away cutting firewood lengths for mid-yard stacks--
awakening old folks from slumbering afternoon naps kept awake
by heard-down-the-block cranked-up radios in tool-filled garages.

For decades families have filled their summer lakeshore cabins,
have driven hours days and nights long distances here for the 4th,
in packed-full vehicles with multi-generations from distant states,
while others have flown airliners cross-country to this sunlit beach;
all make a pilgrimage to a place of sunsets and sandy cold swims;
on cool nights they sleep within the sheets and pulled-up blankets,
between guarding rustic walls under sheltering roofs, keeping out
wildlife roaming among now-shared forest spaces of human dreams.

James R. Ellerston
July 1, 2023

Mid-Summer Good Times

On Nature's Travels

Mother duck and four ducklings swim this early hour
along the beach their early morning voyage all grouped together,
in shallow water near my sandy shore; they move about,
delighting my eyes and heart in the day's new dawning light.

Today's sky has clouds of whiteness floating brightly far above
as distant shores again in greeness emerged in clarity
from weeks of smoking gray-fog obscurity;
things finally look natural again at the lake this early July day.

Visible is a jagged distant tree line across the waters;
it's there beneath pastel shades of soft pink and blue;
there's liquid reflected sky above the purple-edged traveling waves
moving distances toward lapping upon my gentle sloping beach.

Variable light breezes encouraged thoughts of sailing,
and my desire to rig my boat again this season,
and first struggle to stand a silver mast upon her deck in readiness,
to spread white sails against the wind and leave the dock with grace.

A strengthened pole is held stayed in vertical stance by wires so thin,
like challenging things we bravely get through with a network of support;
we're held together by well designed social fabric and adjustments to lines
to get us through the shifting gusts of change throughout our days of life.

At our helm we must choose our direction and make favorable tacks,
not letting ourselves be idly distracted and roughly blown off course,
but following guidelines and rules of the road in encounters with others,
until reaching a safe harbor, with a family eager to venture forth again.

James R. Ellerston
July 3, 2023

Annual Boat Parade 10:00 AM, 4th Of July, 2023

The early morning sun shown on distant green shores
while chipmunks and a gray squirrel scampered about patio concrete
but later have hidden away like the bright rays once shining--
now gone behind an overcast sky of graying clouds
when the temperature has dropped and a wind came up;
we're subjected to a forecast for moisture in later hours.

A sprinkle might make it less inviting to sit out on docks-end chairs
watching a Fourth of July string of boats in a row going past,
and will discourage fun participation by holiday makers in their vessels,
all seeking out independence from schedules or obligations during work,
with time these few long weekend days with family at the lakeside cabin;
our neighbors have traveled hours and distance to be here again together.

In a light shower they sat in yards with umbrellas spread, speakers blaring,
at ten o'clock in anticipation of a parade they hoped would happen today;
still at this hour, there was a joyful mood of celebration in the drizzling air,
after all those miles traveled, hoping it wouldn't really rain on their parade;
boats and flags went by while Lee Greenwood sang-out to the neighborhood;
in joy, I heard the whistle of a steamboat on this lake, coming from the bay.

James R. Ellerston
July 4, 2023

The Morning Of July 6, 2023

Early emergence of fog rising from the water did not please me;
weather the day before had been gray and breezy,
so when today the sun rose beneath a clear blue sky I felt joy
looking out a cabin window at clear views of distant shores.

A veil of mist ascending from the lake was a disappointment;
the temperature of crisp morning air was cool when out for the dog walking
in long sleeves to cover my arms to feel really comfortable;
heat was turned-on inside while I sat in my chair with coffee.

Vaporous clouds rose to nearly treetop height,
swirled about when gusts made patterns on otherwise calm water,
and blocked mirrored reflections on a tranquil surface
while another peaceful day began before company arrived in the evening.

Our calendar was past the summer solstice into the long days of summer;
I hope to swim later today in afternoon before-supper sun;
depths of this water should still be warming each July day--
but I did not swim yesterday in the chilly moving air.

When one sees morning mist there is a quick realization
that lake water is losing heat into the airborne moisture
which evaporates and cools surface liquid after a day of sun heating it;
a swim in late afternoon hours will feel cool, a bit brisk, but still refreshing.

James R. Ellerston
July 6, 2023

This Music Will Go On

A brilliant pianist played a beautiful song to the Facebook world
and his hands sailed upon the keys of white and black,
his notes like waves rushing on the windblown surface of water;
his recording today pulled up "My Heart Will Go On" from my mind.

While he emotionally phrased at the piano with his whole-body dance,
making muscled arm strokes of that chilling night and deathly voyage,
our wet-eye emotions were frozen within that floating tune back then again--
as if we were actually swimming through that melody in time and space.

We remember a brilliant film from decades ago upon our memory's screen--
depicting horror upon an icy ocean shown with a vision for beauty, in a story
of when a strong love had given up a handhold on a buoyant floating door,
and a young man immortalized as "Jack" gave up his own grip and struggle.

With a descending *glissando* down the keys from life,
"Jack" slipped away into a deathly cold deep pitching sea,
but is brought back to life in our human minds
whenever this *requiem eternal* is heard.

James R. Ellerston
July 5, 2023
Michael Andreas Häringer on a Steinway vertical piano July 5, 2023
Song by James Horner with lyrics by Wayne Jennings
James Cameron directed the movie Titanic released in 1997
Celine Dion sang the title song

Being In This Lake Stays With You
For Daeren F. Harp, Age 9

Acrylic goggles from the hardware store,
enabled mornings of true joyful fun,
giving a vision of lake's bottom sands
through the clarity of lens and clear water,
so a growing boy saw snail shells and rocks of interest;
his enclosing and curious hand reached out to their location,
while an inquisitive mind asked for more, "again, again";
he gathered them into a clear plastic dockside dish
to take back home and treasure in his room
after driving to a land of green corn crops and city blight,
where he attended school in an urban place all year--
looking forward to returning to the peaceful cold refreshing beach,
to kick legs and feet and move stronger arms in early morning light,
breathing through a plastic snorkel tube morning cool into lungs,
and spying future reachable objects in his sight within grasp,
which would be in his future slumbering dreams
beneath a blanket's warmth in his secure bed on a winter night.

James R. Ellerston
July 10, 2023

They Played Together At Ten Mile Lake

The big molded dump trucks and pails that grandma procured
were delivered by express from across seas and land;
they now race on the beach making tracks, leaving paths in sand,
and are propelled next to the waves by two small boys enthusiasm
with bare feet and long legs in dripping wet flapping clothes
on lakeshore at a tiny lot with wooden shelters visited for years.

Short child bodies were engines of movement in energetic play--
muscles powered by the sweet starch of breakfast pastries;
bent backs moved colorful plastic as their imaginations directed;
they raised a noise of gleeful fun with shouts and screams;
small plastic wheels clattered over a dock board highway;
an hour passed until winds had chilled both down too cold.

Coffee cup in hand, a nearly exhausted caregiver viewed them,
watching over budding road designers near the water's edge,
where empty of heavy loads hauled on splashing titanic voyages,
sturdy trucks were frequently rescued from windblown lapping surf;
all this is now in my grandsons' memories of our Minnesota lake--
where a 4th generation played together at a lakeshore playground.

James R. Ellerston
July 16, 2023
Bryce A. Romanelli-Gobbi and Liam E. Romanelli-Gobbi played.

Afloat With Liam And Bryce (Tuesday July 18, 2023)

After anticipation for days, all morning, and throughout eating lunch,
we began a boat ride across the smoke obscured lake on a warm day,
starting with a crabby cranking of an obstinate cold engine--
demanding determination to get it firing after a full fueling filled its tank,
then it finally bursting into a smooth idle at dockside;
four passengers boarded with parental strong arms assisting each.

It was now time to back away from the safety of a boat hoist
and head across the smooth waters of the nearly breathless day;
Grandpa guided the boat carefully around the shoreline,
avoiding unmarked rocks and hidden hazards marked with white buoys--
pointing out all to the two small boys and their caregiver mother;
this was the first ride for people to travel on the vessel this season.

They were the first people to sit on the new white vinyl seats
installed earlier in June by their 2nd cousin from Colorado
when he visited Minnesota again after a several year absence;
the runabout plowed, plunging through rough boat wakes of others,
bouncing in their pitching paths of crowded confluence;
avoiding others was a full-time job, and we counted on other's watching too.

On pleasure riding craft, or in an anchored fishing design of shallow draft,
out searching pleasure or for swimming fish from depths beneath and below,
we were out where boaters skimmed the windless, waveless surface,
where a lonely sailboat, with sails limp, sat becalmed in sunshine--
moving ever-so-slowly homeward on an occasional breath of breeze,
like a changing part of the beautiful scenery we beheld from shore.

Our smooth running outboard had powered us back to dockside;
we quickly had a chilly swim in the cold clean waters,
and toweled-off hurriedly to avoid the awful larvae skin itch,
hurrying into warm cabins and a kitchen ready to cook,
for a supper of frozen fish oven-broiled to perfection--
followed by reading the children books before retiring to our beds.

James R. Ellerston   July 19, 2023

Child Of Edinburg, Texas In 1939

It is a photograph of a confident child of 11-12 years maybe,
yet it is an image showing a wholesome family life in detail--
capturing the existence of near poverty in a Texas hut;
there is drabness in a nearly colorless home, but nourishment;
morality is instilled by beliefs in commandments for life on the wall,
ten posted rules remembering Biblical words embracing survival.

A young blond-haired boy looks attentively into a camera's focus;
the sharpness in his vision belies his confidence in life;
work clothing is soiled, but well fitted to his strong form;
the wash basin on the counter tells of kitchen cleanliness;
gallon sized tins from food convey that it is possibly a large family
struggling to survive with a monotonous diet.

The photograph suggests efforts made during depression years;
a mother's touch is seen in the colorful flour-sack curtain
and the dirtied dish towel carefully hung up to dry to his right;
clothes are folded and neatly stacked-up next to the kid;
baking powder, cane syrup, canned milk and salt indicates baking,
utensils with handles in a jar, are near a plate and crockery bowl.

Already large adolescent hands indicates coming to age for war;
he may have been swept to battle in WWII or the Korean conflict,
and might have fought at the front and survived the bitter frostbite;
returning home afterwards the story suggests he might have lived,
enduring life through the polio pandemic of the 1950s,
to possibly raising a family-- little of his future is known.

James R. Ellerston
July 21, 2023
Facebook post Traces of Texas on July 20, 2023 (29.5K Likes in 1 Day)
Photo credited to Russell Lee

When The Car Had Driven Down The Lane

When the rental car had pulled away to the east
and daughter and grandsons had left the lake behind,
family days had run out for this summer season;
until only hopes for holiday get-togethers loomed ahead--
forehead kisses were planted on two dear little boys amid smiles
and silly giggles on their booster seats inside the rear doors.

While well-wishes for safe travels left the grandparents' vocal folds,
emotions were a mixture of love, gratitude, joy and regret,
for time spent embracing growth and new skills learned;
Grandpa had regret for his temper flashing at the young ones;
there was joy at the two boys ability to play together for hours,
racing plastic trucks from Grandma in water and along the beach.

With thankfulness for sharing many blessings of nature's beauty,
the lake toys will be packed away for the coming winter months
in safe but cold storage in the security of the big cabin garage--
between sailboats and under the many beds for sleeping upstairs;
hopes are for more arrivals future summers to this familiar shore--
with four generations, coming to the bare stud and plywood walls.

James R. Ellerston
July 24, 2023

Shadows Of Days They Left Behind

Between two towering huge white pines Grandpa watered as a kid,
underneath their overhanging needled branches of green
on a flat front yard above heaved-up bank and purple blooming plants,
while sheltered from the brightness and heat of midday sun
they made circular outlines, remaining where plastic trucks once roamed.

Amid loud enthusiastic vocalized roars of small boys energetic motors,
driven by vivid imaginations and moved on rounded routes
they delivered hand-shoveled loads of earthen cargo,
leaving behind these marks within the once water-washed sand--
tracks which became startlingly evident shadows in evening's hours.

Golden light from smoke-tinged sun angled down and
prompted a grandparent's rush for a cell phone camera to save electronically
such fragile petroglyphs into the stone of permanent memory of that time--
preserved henceforth for long remembrance of two children's joy and fun
on the days spent with grandparents at the lakeshore cabins.

A week in a friendly neighborhood of people living there for generations--
will be always present in future winter dreams of returning in summers,
for fun times desired in beating hearts, to be part of their remaining days,
even if it takes many hours of travel from distant winter homes
in cities and lands of states far across the nation.

James R. Ellerston
July 25, 2023

A Great Day Begins

For several days there has been clear smokeless air to easily breathe;
and a cloudless blue sky floats above us again this morning;
small ripples on the surface meet my sandy shore;
swirling mist rises from the placid surface,
sucking away water's accumulated heat, upward to treetop height--
a maximum temperature was reached for liquid warmth a few days back.

Today is the last day of July on this year's fleeting calendar,
having reached the halfway point of ninety days of vacation in Minnesota;
this is a lazy summer semester spent at the lake again,
at his favorite place of pleasant visual delight,
where from windows in his comfortable upholstered chair he sees outside--
when the older man sits resting between doing his daily chores.

He hadn't started anything on this early morning time
while watching sunshine rising on the far distant tree-lined bank,
with yellow-green hints of birch and popple within the pine;
closely-spaced docks and boat hoists are visible on treasured beaches
in front of rows of houses stretched along roads for good cabin times--
where sunlight glints and flashes from many reflective panes of glass.

Early morning boaters roar noisily out to fish for fun,
with a goal to bring home a nourishing daily catch;
after a few hours on a rocking hull in the sun of an ever hotter day,
they'll stand in shade cleaning their haul, fry it up, and eat it down the hatch;
meanwhile, I drink my third mug of strong black coffee, planning my work,
what I'll get accomplished today-- but find myself writing poetry instead.

James R. Ellerston
July 31, 2023

Forever

I hate it when you talk about forever--
Like it's in the room watching me eat,
Like it's waiting for me to speak with my mouth full
And my mouth is filled with hesitations,
so I keep chewing
And I keep forever waiting there in the kitchen
Biding its time,
Growing impatient despite its abundance;
And so it hangs there ringing in my ears.
Forever is a jealous lover.

I hate it when you talk about forever--
Like it's a burden, or a cross,
or a stone that one person could bear.
If that one person could bare themselves.
As if we are formidable opponents to eternity in our smallness,
trust me I don't have the callouses for that sort of work.
I am chewing when you ask me if I'll be here for you forever,
And my food gets caught in my throat for what feels like--
Forever is out to get me,
And that's why I hate it when you talk about it.

Stefan Crowl
August 1, 2023
Revision and typescript James R. Ellerston August 15, 2023

Big Waves Crashing In The Storm

There is a beauty in the passing of a storm,
this is felt in heart and soul,
in a building we safely sleep in beds tonight,
our slumbers kept within these wooden walls.

With big waves crashing on this beach
In a golden fireball of a setting sun,
white foam crested water-trapped-wind racing to me--
an energy visible to eyes and heard by ears
moving through the water toward my shore.

There is a beauty in the passing of a storm,
this is felt in relief of heart and soul,
in a building we safely sleep in beds tonight,
our slumbers kept within these wooden walls.

Just a gentle rumble of low thunder,
and bright glare of lightning's flash
while rain splashes noisily window panes of glass
and droplets patter on rooftop sheltering sheets;
this storm progresses across the land and clouds march on.

There is a beauty in the passing of a storm,
this is felt in relief of heart and soul,
in a building we safely sleep in beds tonight,
our slumbers kept within these wooden walls.

At morning's early light with darkness come and gone,
after nighttime hours slept away in restful slumber,
and air cleared of smoke showing clearly distant views--
green treed banks now visible for miles across our lake,
while baby ducklings swim with no danger between dock posts.

There is a beauty in the passing of a storm,
this felt in relief of heart and soul
in a building we safely sleep in beds tonight,
our slumbers kept within these wooden walls.

James R. Ellerston   August 2-3, 2023

Between Lake And Lawn

We're looking out our window panes at flowers on the banks--
purple blossoms on climbing plants of green, so tall they stand;
nestled amongst rocks and sand along these valued shores,
on this transition from water to land, this gentle sloping beach
between wave-swept lake and green-grown grass of lawns.

The beauty of a hot calm dawn with little moving breeze--
there's dry air and sunshine and lack of choking smoke;
this makes our breathing easier but we're still feeling lazy
these otherwise productive times of tasks,
with little or nothing motivating us and little work we've done,
throughout the passing of another summer season's day.

We're looking out our window panes at flowers on the banks--
purple blossoms on climbing plants of green, so tall they stand;
nestled amongst rocks and sand along these valued shores,
on this transition from water to land, this gentle sloping beach
between wave-swept lake and green-grown grass of lawns.

An evening boat parade begins its nightly voyage--
crowded vessels loaded with many pairs of shaded eyes sail past;
with drinks in hands they search our cabins for designs,
to see what other folks not unlike them might possess,
how people meet lake life's challenges and tasks
in the later moments of their lifetime hours.

We're looking out our window panes at flowers on the banks--
purple blossoms on climbing plants of green, so tall they stand;
nestled amongst rocks and sand along these valued shores,
on this transition from water to land, this gentle sloping beach
between wave-swept lake and green-grown grass of lawns.

Low rumbling engines slowly move with blue smoking dignity--
unlike urgent youth they are not hurried and roaring fast;
keeping a distance from my shallow depths and dock as they pass,
observing that some would swim within these warmed-up waters,
brief moments in late afternoon before supper's hunger beckons
some to cook fish busily in an iron pan, or on a propane grill.

We're looking out our window panes at flowers on the banks--
purple blossoms on climbing plants of green, so tall they stand;
nestled amongst rocks and sand along these valued shores,
on this transition from water to land, this gentle sloping beach
between wave-swept lake and green-grown grass of lawns.

James R. Ellerston
August 3, 2023

A Wee Song With Singing Smiles

(It's in the) quiet hours of early waking morning
(before) trucks and cars on roads so noisily roar
(that the) loons' cries echo across these waters
(sounding) all is well at this lake shore.

(And her) head's still dozing on her pillow
(she has) slept past dark times dreaming through
(and we'll) soon fry-up eggs and cook fat sausages
(work outside) in this blessed yard and house.

(It's in the) quiet hours of early waking morning
(before) trucks and cars on roads so noisily roar
(that the) loons' cries echo across these waters
(sounding) all is well at this lake shore.

(This is where) families came for generations
(together) sat down for meals eaten with God's grace
(they've given) thanks for what farm and forest gave them
(and these) warm summer months at their lakeside place.

(It's in the) quiet hours of early waking morning
(before) trucks and cars on roads so noisily roar
(that the) loons' cries echo across these waters
(sounding) all is well at this lake shore.

(At daybreak) after moonbeams glow, through rainy cloudy nights
(it's in) golden rays of brightening sun, shining warmly in our sights
(and when we're) rested work for hours, toiling in bright hot lights
(in the days) of summer ahead, with family we swim and play.

(It's in the) quiet hours of early waking morning
(before) trucks and cars on roads so noisily roar
(that the) loons' cries echo across these waters
(sounding) all is well at this lake shore.

(If we lay) minutes stretched-out on a towel, searching for a moist skin tan
(not just letting) years pass by aging older, while becoming a lady or a man
(after times with) a chosen lover wed, brought here children of our own,
(and during) years of raising a family, never sat and ate alone.

(It's in the) quiet hours of early waking morning
(before) trucks and cars on roads so noisily roar
(that the) loons' cries echo across these waters
(sounding) all is well at this lake shore.

(So when we) ask you to go to the cabin, to share our walls and beds
(do pack your) car and drive Up-North with us, not work your job instead
(by car or) plane please come be with us, where in scenery we've been led
(and if Dad) declines to grill burned food, at least you'll be well fed.

(It's in the) quiet hours of early waking morning
(before) trucks and cars on roads so noisily roar
(that the) loons' cries echo across these waters
(sounding) all is well at this lake shore.

(Oh we've been) driving to this forest land, for nearly seventy years
(many times on) choked busy roads, trips for pleasure it appears
(sometimes we'd) meet new folks here, who'd travel from states away
(who'd journeyed) far to return each year, for long weekends or holidays.

(It's in the) quiet hours of early waking morning
(before) trucks and cars on roads so noisily roar
(that the) loons' cries echo across these waters
(sounding) all is well at this lake shore.

(Oh these are) lonely times for me now, without friends around a corner;
(I no longer) know people at this place, some have died and live no more
(Young children) happily play on beaches, driving toys in water and on sand
(but they too) so soon went home, leaving me an empty cabin in this land.

(It's in the) quiet hours of early waking morning
(before) trucks and cars on roads so noisily roar
(that the) loons' cries echo across these waters
(sounding) all is well at this lake shore.

(but too soon)Autumn's leaves drop down, we pack away our sailing toys
(and in fall) docks come apart, are stacked by crews of muscled boys
(fair weather)boats find shed's sheltering steel, trailer cradles are berths
(and we'll go) south for working winter months, to earn our cabin's worth.

(It's in the) quiet hours of early waking morning
(before) trucks and cars on roads so noisily roar
(that the) loons' cries echo across these waters
(sounding) all is well at this lake shore.

(We'll sing) music on cold bitter nights, strum guitars in winds and snows
(we garland) houses with bright lights, colored balls, and boughs of green
(somehow we) survive long dark months, by cozy hearths and fire's warmth;
(and when) trees leaf out in early spring, start dreaming again of going North.

(It's in the) quiet hours of early waking morning
(before) trucks and cars on roads so noisily roar
(that the) loons' cries echo across these waters
(sounding) all is well at this lake shore.

James R. Ellerston
August 4,5,6, 2023

From Glenn's Photos He Took While Traveling

Cattle graze lush green fields
on a bright and beautiful day;
seedheads of grasses wave in wind,
on gently rolling pasture land along a country river bank;
the long horizon beneath earth and heavens stretches
in a distant line of sight on our long paths
between black fertile soils and cloud-sailed blue seas above.

There are few trees growing along the water,
with other craggy bare remnants of previous growth and death;
lush groves of farmsteads are at fields' edges,
and surviving small towns at distant ends of farm views sprout;
the feeding animals are both brown and black
spread out along the meandering creek bed,
lighter colored beasts rest, off their feet, laying on the ground.

Sunshine warms cattle's backs,
no shade outdoors when moving there;
blue skies are filled with moving wispy clouds
driven by steady breezes on their gentle passages;
they fill our bright sights with pleasure
in their daily voyages across the heavens
on trips along daylight and dark nights' paths.

Small stones crunch beneath our car tire;
bees hurry in their search for pollen,
hurrying to trips between roadside blossoms
and flowered ground surrounding structures for storing grain;
soybean leaves whisper in the morning breeze;
tall tasseled-out corn plants rattle on the opposite side
as we drive country gravel roads from farm to town today.

James R. Ellerston   August 16, 2023
Photos by Glenn Henriksen also from February 15, 2023

Toddler's Final Journey On Governor Abbott's Orders

Guards had stood over them and others like them
and loaded them all on board with others like them;
their destination was unknown to those poor souls now departing,
all they knew was they were unwanted people where they were,
and were being sent somewhere further along in a hate-filled world;
now party politics moved them on;
that's something Texas law allowed.

Wheels turned beneath their conveyance,
they were jostled by bumps and curves;
hopes were for a better future than that left behind;
it had been a long desert journey already;
hunger had traveled with them;
once they'd hoped for future safety,
not a life with pointing guns.

Her parents had safely held her tenderly,
for all that way, traversing many borders,
while they crossed the unknown distances and regions,
for days in heat and dark night miles, to now roll on in blackness;
she had grown ever weaker and a loving mother comforted her;
finally they were allowed to leave the coach,
when an Illinois hospital took her nearly dead body in.

Then it was just too late, no medicine could cure neglectful harm--
days of withheld doctors' care, just water and food instead;
those big Texans did not want her folks or race around
in their hate-filled state of those self-deemed superior;
and this little toddler had left this spiteful world behind--
and only weeping folks remain,
now she has died and traveled to regions beyond.

James R. Ellerston
August 20, 2023

Texas confirmed the 3-year-old child's death. Illinois Department of Public Health said the child died Thursday August 17, 2023 in Marion County in southern Illinois where the child had received treatment from paramedics and later was pronounced dead at a hospital, one of four deaths of "migrant" children this year. She was two weeks shy of age four. Jismary Alejandra Barboza Gonzalez
was born in Colombia to Venezuelan parents. They had crossed through Panama, Costa Rica, Nicaragua, Honduras, and Guatemala before Mexico, waiting there two months of appointments to seek asylum to no avail. Held in US government custody for three days she was bussed from Brownsville, Texas as part of Abbott's plan to traffic people to Chicago. The plan is to simply leave them on the sidewalk after promising housing and work.

Song For Alan (Takatsuka)

You'd all been there once before,
On a visit to my famous town
Before hot fires burned Lahaina down
Turned my boyhood home into ash and coals
Hot flames came and it was gone,
But the famous tree did grow on
It received water and care, and a world in prayer,
All hoped the Banyan Tree would survive.

They smelled the smoke,
They felt the heat-- the cool ocean waters some sought;
There was just this one road to get them out;
They followed that car in front,
So slow it drove, the line so long,
They prayed they'd kept moving along;
They had no choice but to leave,
There was just one way to stay alive that day.

Maui had been his boyhood home,
Now he has only memories carrying on;
They will build back the town;
It'll rise again he knows;
He'll say Hawaii is his home for the remainder of his days;
Some had had enough, and flew from this paradise;
airplanes left with survivors' lives,
a few hundred already had died.

In his youthful growing years
he'd lived there on that beach,
until he met his gal of dreams
and went to a prairie town to teach;
but each summer they'd go back home,
to see parents, family, and hang around;
for months on that island shore,
their home was in that Hawaian town.

James R. Ellerston
August 25, 2023
Alan and Debby Takatsuka were teachers at Senior High School in Fort Dodge, Iowa, and were summering in Lahaina when the fire hit the town in 2023.
Fort Dodge Messenger   http:// www. messengernews.net/ news/local-news/ 2023/08/narrow-escape-2
Facebook Post Debby Takatsuka on August 23, 2023? "I have tried so many times to post this" August 19, 2023?

We Are Warned Of Cold That's Coming

These strong winds blow,
      making their gust patterns on the water;
whistling wind is in the trees,
      rattling leaves upon their swaying forest branches;
one hopes for sun's warmth,
      as gray clouds sail like ships on futile voyages;
I hold my coffee mug,
      filled with hot alertness in my hand.

Sunlight moves along the shorelines
      shining on the distant docks and houses there;
light peaks beneath the clouds
      underneath laden moisture-filled heavens;
I plan my day after putting refuse out
      then make a town-trip for groceries;
several naps will fill my idle hours giving needed sleep
      giving eyes rest in a dark room.

I must get moving
      and actually accomplish some tasks in these hours;
so I'll take a walk today,
      work moving about the cabin;
maybe I should mow the lawn,
      it's time the wildflowers are cut down and stalks are raked;
it's time the yard looks sharp, it is fall approaching now,
      we'll all drive south, leaving vacant cabins beneath the snow.

A chipmunk on my step
      teases at my window to challenge my puppy dog;
birds fly their courses aloft
      from one branch to another for chosen landing sites;
to exercise our bodies
      we'll assist others with tasks and challenges;
helping move some along their paths,
      and we'll get through our lives together.

There is much to do before we pack the car,
    and heavily loaded down go to prairie lands;
that's where waves don't splash and crash upon sand
    on my own personal beach;
each day I swim and bathe in the lake,
    soaping my body and upon my hair put shampoo;
vacations cleanse our minds,
    should make us feel better, and survive the long winter.

For now I'll play and sing,
    make music with friends we'll meet and know;
at home I am a church choir member
    sitting in the organ loft for others for an anthem;
eyes located on our faces look out the world
    from a driven searching mind inside;
we count aging in calendar years, days of youthful bodies,
    quickening middle-aged, galloping decades toward death.

James R. Ellerston
August 27, 2023

Feed And Water Daily

Tiny drops on the window
        have dried from the wind;
Wet tears in my eyes
        watered the tissue of my face;
Creeping loss of muscle strength
        still allows me to labor and play;
Fog in my mind
        obscures my thoughts;
Angered moments have wasted time, sleep, and appetite
        and destroyed chances for expression;
Because of my anger
        I am unable to see beauty in daily life.

Pain in my heart
        has blocked my love, my verse, and creativity;
Growing hope in my soul
        continues to carry me on;
Strong faith in your future
        encourages me to always care for you;
Constant criticism stifles me
        until I have no self-worth to express;
My belief in your strength
        cause me to rely on you;
Stupid ignorance keeps me from choosing to do what's right
        even though I'd always like to.

James R. Ellerston
August 27, 2023

Doing Dishes

With my hands immersed into the soapy liquid
I felt for the revered old china heirloom dish;
the water was not excessively hot,
but washing dishes was my next least favorite thing--
that is after grocery shopping.

I'm good at cleaning dishware, pans, and silverware,
and scrub all of it really clean;
in hard rusty well water it's hard to get a shine,
but with a tea towel one can wipe a lot off
and get the dry surfaces almost bare.

A lot depends on the detergent used,
and whether it's appropriate for long sink soakings;
sometimes I let them all sit for days--
the bottom of the basin littered with old food smells;
I might get the sink emptied and scoured by closing-up time.

James R. Ellerston
August 29, 2023

Fall Bombing From Oak Trees
(For My Sister And Brother-In-Law)

Sharp taps awaken our slumbers on a near sleepless night;
"pops" keep our dogs alert peering-out with protective sight;
oak trees drop their acorns in this changing season
like bombardiers doing carpet bombing of our world.

They intend no harm from these missiles of procreation;
a few are left defused by squirrels who crack most of them open,
leaving pieces of gaping shells strewn about the ground
from devouring the inner seeds of each.

No trees will fill the forest from this satisfaction of hunger,
or the gathering and storage by these busy animals
about their tasks each day like factory workers;
acorns land upon roofs, cars, boats, and campers.

Any metal makes a loud noise at each crash upon its surface;
it's amazing this organic hailing does not pock-mark surfaces;
this continues through the earliest weeks of changing leaves in fall;
before snows fall quietly compared to this autumnal bombardment.

James R. Ellerston
August 30, 2023

Last Mid-afternoon Visit With Shirley 2023

She was getting ready to leave the lake for home;
her oval rug was rolled-up halfway across the shining wooden floor;
she seemed obsessed with the final packing process,
preoccupied with all the details of closing-up a cabin--
shutting down this summer home for the harsh winter ahead,
and doing things correctly so there would be an easy spring time return;
I suggested she take a break from her energetic working,
so she did and spent a few moments conversing with me.

She sat with restful poise upon her sofa near her writing materials and books
and we both gazed-out through the glazing at the weather and the water,
at the dark clouds relentlessly moving across the sky--
both of us regretting the cold temperatures of the windy overcast day;
I wore my new warm Ten Mile Lake sweatshirt for the first time,
modeling the gray soft fabric and the lettering across the chest;
one of her antique clocks chimed its stately tolling with a rich tone;
she checked her wrist watch and announced it was time to get her dinner.

I read-out only six lines from my poetry notebook to her and headed home;
she would eat a solitary evening meal and routinely retire early;
at my cabin I'd catch the brief twenty moments of sun that shone and swim,
scrubbing-up a few beach toys for months of garage storage;
I would nap away an hour of afternoon leisure under a warm comforter,
and sit down and push my wordy pen across the paper's surface
recording this September Saturday of my own hurried tasks
and my regret for a farewell that would extend for long months elsewhere.

James R. Ellerston
September 16, 2023

Lending Libraries

I would like a world without censorship,
    of free thinking, and freedom to read anything;
I would like a world of knowledge
    with no book burners, flaming cauldrons, or destructive pyres;
I would like to read a book
    that says the world is not flat;
I would like to read a book
    that says the earth revolves with other planets around its sun;
I would like to read a book
    that gives characters a choice of the race of persons to love;
I would like a book that states they did not have a right
    to seize my land for their money-making schemes;
I would like a book that states they did not have a right
    to forbid a culture, deny a language, and falsify a history;
I would like a book that says
    no human king is God ordained to rule;
I would like a book that says
    no one system of government is superior to another;
I would like a book that says
    no human race is superior to another;
I would like a book that says
    one can be the citizen of a nation despite a mother's religion;
I would like a book that says they had no right to return and seize
    land because they read it an ancient religious text;
I would like to read a book that says they have no right
    to criminalize my choice of the sexuality of a person I love;
I would like to read that there is no legality in criminalizing
    my creation of works of art, music, drama, poetry, or prose;
I would like to read that there is no legality in denying me life
    due to financial inability to buy and pay for medicine or care.

James R. Ellerston
September 21, 2023

On My Nearly Empty Lakeside Street

At summer's end dry brown oak leaves are blowing down;
Noisily falling acorns are scattered about the ground;
There's a real need to rake the yard today,
Little lake time remains to just rest or play.

So many year-end tasks listed to hurry and do;
No time to postpone them and sit and stew;
Four days left here before south I'll drive,
Going home for winter month's activities to stay alive.

I'll keep up on politics, world events, and warring strife;
And try to minimize my health issues and enjoy family life;
When those cold dark months of winter snow are done,
Back north to our shoreside neighborhood we'll come for fun.

James R. Ellerston
September 21, 2023

On Friday September 22, 2023

Three white seagulls fished the lake's surface waters
in an area where Autumn's golden leaves reflected, while
two gulls were on quiet waters without shimmers from breezes;
on this warm morning the opening day of fall, birds sang in trees;
cabin-closing tasks preoccupied thoughts even sitting resting,
after working at yet another thing keeping myself busy.

I have three days left on my remaining to-do lists
before the car is loaded going to Iowa with nothing missed;
after final choices of what to keep from the freezer and fridge,
there are lots of strange meals using-up things each day;
I make decisions of what to transport home or to throw-away,
reading use-by dates deciding what to discard or keep and take.

Squirrels and chipmunks scurry about for what can be found;
geese honk-out their southward navigation flying below clouds;
a pet dog's yard-visits accumulate Milkbones upon the carpet;
coffee in a mug warms morning inspiring thoughts on paper set;
I will clean-up yards, with shoes on, pruning clippers in my hand,
making decisions which trees to cut, or another season to stand.

James R. Ellerston
September 22, 2023

My Last Saturday On Our Shore For 2023

On this pewter gray misty day heavens were overcast with clouds
and rippled water gently lapped along the sandy shoreline,
I had slept late into daylight hours in my dark warm bedroom
heated by an electric heater unit on a wall near my feet.

A cold northeast breeze whistled in the trees,
feeling uncomfortably cool in early morning against my bare legs;
I put jeans on and safely started loading food into the shaded car,
and luggage from second story bedrooms was carried down.

This is the day to move about in a crawl space beneath the kitchen
scooting on my bum at ladder's bottom, draining pipes into sand,
opening valves to let the water freely flow out, with the power off,
warm water from the heater was drained out for the year.

My guest cabin will be closed-down for coming winter months,
paintings covered to safely shelter from bitter storms;
there are long lists of myriad things during these final days
and after hot coffee, and cream cheese on crackers, I'll do work.

The peace of a pileated woodpecker resting on his sturdy branch,
was disturbed by the ascent of a gray squirrel up a pine trunk--
scurrying at high speed up the vertical side of my front yard tree;
repeated bird flights indicated this sandy airport was open today.

James R. Ellerston
September 23, 2023

In Pella For
A Fun Week

Joe Played Wonderfully At Alumni Pans

He played so well on his guitar routines that day
moving about the platform and guitar neck with skill and grace,
performing songs with a youthful agility,
and rhythmic footwork reflecting his concentration.

He expressed a sense of musical phrasing with his gentle dance,
legs and feet sometimes simply moving or tapping-out the beat;
as he worked the forestage in black athletic shoes
dressed in slim-legged red pants, flowing T shirt, wearing a smile.

He played such singing liquid musical lines
or quick improvisations within the changing chords;
he's good at his game of tossing musical ideas back and forth;
relaxed arm movement strummed responsive "distorted" patterns.

Accentuating motives brought out melodic passages,
while he played with a maturity of balance and creativity;
when he moved to the back court he drummed out his playing
on the great barrel pans in moves basic to the harmonic changes.

He's a master of his style on the solo work up high,
sometimes matched-up working with another player as a pair
and doubling ideas within his musical units as a duet;
but today he was so much a part of a larger team.

The stage was filled with more than a dozen steel-pan players;
each did their part so the ensemble would win their game,
and perform well in this Homecoming Concert on stage that day;
many traveled miles to participate with players from other years.

James R. Ellerston   October 2, 2023
Central College Alumni Pans rehearsed Sept. 30 and Oct. 1, 2023
Joe Roberts graduated from Central with a history major in 2021.

More
Poems From
My Daughter's
Teenage Years

Peace

The far-off whine of a police siren
pierces the air in a neighborhood;
What troubles we have today!
Blood on the sidewalk,
paint on the walls,
war in Sarajevo--
Will the troubles ever end?

Hunger stalks,
starving people try to keep living,
gangs roam out on the streets,
rebellion is in their minds;
Somewhere someone cries-out--
their mind is sore for something else
called 'peace'.

Julia K. Ellerston
Sometime in the 1996-97 school year
Edited James R. Ellerston November 24, 2023

Wake

Scorched grass says 'goodbye' to fallen children
frozen in warful death for nothing;
Sorrowful angry tears spill over
the rims of eyes of black-clothed mourners;
Children are dying morbid deaths in the silence
of mortar shells raining death and destruction;
Enemies are surrounding others
with allies strong and many--
to strangle the innocent and feeble.

Monstrous guns shoot to kill innocent bystanders
wishing war was never there--
was never real;
Masses of bloodied people with reaching arms--
are reaching-out to be carried away to safety;
women cry-out to be rescued;
mothers beg to the rescuers,
"Take my child to safety for me,
rescue my child from this massacre."

Julia K. Ellerston
Sometime in the 1996-97 school year
Edited James R. Ellerston November 24, 2023

Where Raindrops Fall

Where raindrops fall
there is peace for all,
and grass and flowers grow--
where everything is green and alive
and bees are buzzing 'round their hive.

Where raindrops fall
everything is all rosy and keen;
it's where war is fiction and life is serene;
there's something exciting occurring every day,
where showing the path also lights up the way.

Julia K. Ellerston
Sometime in the 1996-97 school year
Edited James R. Ellerston November 24, 2023

Old Glory

The banner hangs limp,
with ragged edges
as the people march
to war.

Its stripes and stars
are muddy
and bloody
from the fighting of men.

It was shot by the redcoats,
and holes from bayonets
pierced the bedraggled cloth
of the new country's flag.

Julia K. Ellerston
Sometime in the 1996-97 school year
Edited James R. Ellerston November 24, 2023

Daydream

Quiet serenity,
no sounds, no noises,
no distractions or disturbances,
total peace.

I lay in the grass
smelling fresh-cut sweetness;
I bury my thoughts in a hole in the ground,
surrounded by the green.

Feelings fly away
like blackbirds,
swift, swift, but still;
all is quiet.

Silent bluebell eyes stare
into the face of the fading sky
as night spreads her gentle twilight veil
upon the sun's fair face.

Stars now shine,
like cookie-cutter punch-outs;
stars shedding a shallow light
upon my face.

Julia K Ellerston
Sometime in the 1996-97 school year
Edited by James R. Ellerston November 24, 2023

Fall October Trip
To Thomat
In Wisconsin

View On A Rainy October Day

Outside the windows gravesite flags wave in the yard
where flowers still grow above the lake;
the plants survived the summer months near the granite stones,
one where a veteran is buried on this gently rising shore,
a brass plaque upon his memorial faces toward the water
on the high bank's slope with his bride's marker near.

They loved this view across these watery depths,
the tree covered hills beyond the surface shimmer;
inside we cannot hear the branches blowing in the breeze,
within these sturdy well-built wall where families worked together
and played on bright summer days in the spring-fed swimming pool
and swam in warmth and pleasure in the sun.

They watched generations of their children grow as years passed,
until grandparents they'd become themselves;
and at death family may decide to put more ashes in this place too;
this is a place where flags will always wave in a yard,
and memorial flowers grow above this beautiful lake.

James R. Ellerston
October 6, 2023

Our Saturday Morning in Wisconsin

Early I walk the dog in bright morning sun
when with dew upon wet grass he frolics and has fun;
golden leaves are above us on light filtered trees,
and flutter down about the ground and our feet;
moving morning air blows against my legs.

I am still wearing shorts from my long night of dreaming,
I haven't yet had breakfast with planning work and schemes;
but now my spoon scrapes my plastic yogurt cup
and after biscuits and two cups of coffee I've had enough,
and will do some reading and move my pen across the page.

Through windows' glass I look about at waters return reflections,
at colored trees and breeze-blown shimmering patterns;
we enjoy our times here in this beautiful spot--
it's a higher elevation than life at our winter home,
and in fall has a beauty and temperatures not as warm.

My wife and I always enjoy our days here,
for "Grandma's house in the woods" is somewhere dear;
we're motivated to drive the long hours and many miles,
searching for a better way with fewer cities and less traffic;
when we get there, forest beauty prompts everyday smiles.

James R. Ellerston
October 8, 2023

The Dog Wanted Out Again

My dog wanted out once more and I stepped into the yard;
sparkling dew covered wet grass;
dampness was beneath my cold bare feet;
a cool wind blew against my chilled body.

In the darkness of the night I saw the moon in a clear sky,
and by early morning I saw sun rising in the East;
enough leaves were down to see the sun now through the woods
as it climbed skyward across the neighbors field.

To our northeast I saw their new house up on the hill
where I heard geese honk in the yard at dawn's light;
yet it was still bitter each time the dog wanted out,
and I tried to hurry him along to do his business.

And again I climbed back into my large warm bed,
and tried to feel some remaining body heat to slumber,
for a few more hours away beneath a decades-old sleeping bag,
until I could feel my warm feet touch each other again.

James R. Ellerston
October 10, 2023

That Day At Thomat

Quiet here permeated the woods,
a gray sky was partly cloudy,
and the even light was gently on the eyes;
shadows were soft on the leaf strewn ground;
no breeze drove trees in wild dance--
just a gentle occasional movement was at branches' tips.

If it was early and there was no noise of machines,
no hammering from the adjoining neighbor's construction,
no chainsaws viciously logging mature trees for greedy profit;
our dog had ceased his morning barking for his biscuits,
had made his business trips into the grassy yard,
and again slept at my wife's feet while she silently slumbered.

Her breakfast she had postponed until later,
and morning hours marched away without her eating yet;
no yogurt cup was emptied for licking-out by our eager pet;
no warm cup of blended tea was brewed in her favorite mug;
it would be a slow easy day today at our forest house;
a simple routine sandwich would nourish us throughout that day.

James R. Ellerston
October 10, 2023

Photogenic

There was no breeze on the lake this morning
and reflection of the clouds was clear'
sun shone on the leaves on the far banked hill
and trees' colors were mirrored upon the surface;
all this waiting for the shutter of my cell phone camera.

Morning started out so sunny and yet cool,
later clouding over so that shadows were indistinct;
nearer to lunch time sunshine re-emerged,
leaves lit up in vibrant colors out windows' views;
the day had warmed-up so the dog's yard visit was a pleasure.

It's beautiful outside here in the Wisconsin woods,
even more so when the sun shines through,
but it has been cloudy here and cold;
I sit inside and enjoy the clear glass transparency,
thankful for the warmth and nighttime sound of a furnace roaring.

James R. Ellerston
October 11, 2023

Last Evening's Supper

Four had sat at a round table near the window
that night gathered together in the local Inn;
one young man explained he'd been there with his grandmother;
the other guy seemed reluctant about the menu prices
until the older man, the host, set a limit on what they could spend--
so the boy felt free to order something he'd like to eat..

They sat around each other while they dined;
the man and wife sat across from each other
while explaining the restaurant's history from previous times--
how it had been a single room in such a simple house,
until it was now expanded with style and elegance;
here they had passed together some precious evening hours.

Love shown at that table flowed back and forth between them all,
in conversational tone, nodding heads, and focused eyes;
attentive ears and minds shared topics of discussion;
but the honest evidence of real communication and affection
was the cashier's question as the gray-haired man paid the ticket,
and she asked, "Are those two young guys your grandsons?"

James R. Ellerston
October 12, 2023
Auston Olson and Brok Hathaway are two friends in Wisconsin

In The Night

When I had stepped outside as "Bravo" asked,
it was with an anxious pet into the yard;
the sky was a velvet black in the night,
bejeweled with stars twinkling bright,
and one was almost startled with that sight
of such unexpected beauty on an unpredictable trip.

Later when my dog signaled for another visit on the grass,
and I ventured forth into even colder breezy air,
there were no longer visible sparkes in a cloudy sky,
but an aircraft moved across instead with a moving white light,
making a trip from here to there in flight;
I hurried into furnace's warmth and back into my bed.

By early afternoon leaves floated about the lake,
voyaging from here to there for our visual delight;
it was the breeze that propelled them on the water;
we saw them at noon during sandwich making time,
and felt sun's warmth while viewing, holding plates and dining,
each joy usually astounded us simply at our casual finding.

James R. Ellerston
October 12, 2023

A Grove Of Tree Poems

A Grove Of Tree Poems

I.
What is it about a Sycamore tree in a gap in Northumberland?
once it was an iconic piece of the North East of England
which some had the pleasure to see twice in their lifetime;
there was something deeply spiritual about it--
poignant and captivating each time visited
but cut down as a pointless prank by an unfeeling nothing,
the stump left a hole in persons' hearts;
this isolated tree once strongly stood near Hadrian's Wall.

II.

A Banyan Tree grew on Maui in the city of Lahaina
in the distant Hawaiian Islands chain;
after winds and fire engulfed the area
and the beach town town burned to ashes on the ground,
people asked about its survival;
persons who'd traveled from around the world
had seen this multi-acre growing wonder made of wood,
standing out amongst the plastic world of souvenir shops;
after the flames big trucks hauled in loads of fresh water
and spread moisture on the ground around its roots
as the world hoped and some prayed
that it would live to be strong and sound again.

III.
Between our two Wisconsin family cabins by a lake
grows this massive needled tree;
one sees its huge trunk of such great girth
and stand in its shade by sunlit day
and amid its moving shadows
from outdoor floodlights on windy nights;
I'm each year even more amazed at its survival.

IV.

Only in one city through which we drive
is there still a great arched canopy across the highway;
a few great Elms survived the tree disease at great expense
and their branches still touch above us,
now waving in the breeze from our passing traffic
as State Highway 15 passes between their trunks,
and we are always amazed at how cities might have one appeared
before Dutch fungus came killing elms, sweeping across the land.

V.

Outside my Iowa farmhouse bedroom window
a Silver maple had grown for many years,
providing leafy shade from hot noonday sun in my room
and shadows moving across my desktop page;
until I returned home for that saddened time,
to find that my father had cut it down
because it was so close to the old house.

VI.

The city had cut those shading trees all over town,
fearing damage if diseased they'd fallen on structures or cars;
now the ash were no more near his house
and he's no longer making 7th Avenue North his home;
after chainsaws bitter bite and raucous sound
his eyes became moist, his tears dripped on stumps and ground;
but the young man that I know, moved on, and lived his life.

VII.

Roads diverged as we drove hundreds of miles,
arriving at a forest house in a yellowed wood;
great needled trees still green and tall,
white barked trunks in groves stood proudly;
leaves in all colors had fallen and scattered about the lawn,
or were visible along blacktops when driving the distance to town;
we steered our car on twisty curves with care,
and even though we're from a prairie state,
found ourselves relieved by straighter highways through fields;
some were harvested, others awaited the giant combines.

VIII.

After hours of driving southward and westward too,
we finally arrived at our winter house in Pella, Iowa;
and found such a surprise with many plants still green;
most leaves still clung to their branches aloft,
only a few had fallen onto lawns still growing;
also there were blooming flowers yet in outdoor beds;
but close listening heard few birds about,
yet squirrels run rampant about the yards and parks;
property owners are pruning their trees,
hopefully months before winter snows begin to fly.

IX.

We'd gone and played outdoors together our cowboy games,
my sister and I in our tree by the "crick" on the stream bank
just down the hill a bit from our house;
it officially has the same name as our township,
and that was always pronounced "Jack Creeeek".

A big Cottonwood tree had stood there on the slope;
within its sheltering timbers we'd spent hours
surround by the multiple upward arching branches;
we sat in the safety of the flat cavernous space within;
it was a favorite place of childhood joy.

Then came a time the county board did us wrong;
in their zeal to improve the drainage of the ditch
they came along all those scenic wooded windbreak shores
and cut all the trees down, now forever gone from views;
bare land replaced the shaded pasture where our tree had grown.

X.

My wife and I had lived in our house forty years
and always enjoyed the great silver maple in our front yard,
and the red-leafed maple with the slightly damaged trunk--
the tree itself in good condition except that area--
there was no bark there, a scar faced the street.

We moved away from that city to another town
at a time young people did not want to have mature trees--
did not want to care for the autumn leaves dropping down;
so the new owner cut our beloved trees to ugly stumps,
cleared away yew and cedars to operate a riding lawnmower.

James R. Ellerston
Oct. 14, 20, Nov. 4, 2023

We Returned
To Pella
For The Fall

Met Central College Friends That Afternoon

My first day back from Wisconsin I saw friends again,
walking across the campus by pond's western end,
he proudly with his wife at his side;
both had attended college here,
I'd met them when they were still students;
he had gone to the flute class recital to hear her play.

Once he had driven our car back from a Des Moines airport flight
when we'd first moved our home to Pella to live;
Facebook had been the medium I used to follow his Navy career
as he moved around the country from San Diego to Georgia;
he worked at teaching languages and I utilized Messenger
on my cell phone to arrange for our brief time today.

The three of us met and stood together on a concrete sidewalk
under our nation's flag waving on the tall pole nearby;
it was such a brief exchange-- a hello, handshake, hug;
a short time to converse before an appointment elsewhere;
we talked about the town of Oskaloosa where he'd once lived,
just down the highway where my ancestors had long ago dwelled.

James R. Ellerston
October 18, 2023
Efrain Garcia is in the U.S. Navy

Scenes Of Fall In Glenn's Photos

These scenes of fall with a bright sky above
provided correct lighting for the lens of a camera
on a beautiful sunshiny day to take pictures
that people later admired and commented about.

Naked tree branches shone in the golden light
under the matte evenness of clouded heavens
while shadows stretched across the fields of stalks;
black bark of a single cottonwood contrasted with the brightness.

Geometric patterns in the railroad bridge spanned the river valley;
a low held viewpoint showed shining grasses waving
near the state highway and along the river waters' banks,
under even tones of a gilded horizon above fertile farms.

Shadowed rows of crop stubble patterned a field
under contrasts of light and shadow on harvested land
outside the bare sheltering trees of an Iowa town
at workday's end when all was at evening's rest.

A single spruce was caught in a view of a distant grain elevator
over a carefully mown cemetery lawn;
a standing crop of corn awaited the combine and
reminded alert viewers of work to be done before winter snows.

A herd of cattle foraged in a harvested field
searching out grain left behind by the giant gleaning machine;
they're given these weeks to roam freely in a larger space
before winter's close confinement in a farmer's feed lot.

Dried stems of grass wave in the blowing breezes--
these thin twisted tubes which survived the summer season
stand stalwart throughout the winds of autumn in fence lines
or along rain-rutted routes to market for bountiful crops.

A grove of old cemetery trees lifts life's promise up
from the gravestones of a rural graveyard,
once the pride of a country church now gone;
worshippers who attend services in town continue burials here.

Under golden leaves clinging to their branches of life,
older buildings lean their frames into lives of constant decline;
some find new purposes in current times, others are weathered
and aged to a point of end readiness to collapse into final demise.

James R. Ellerston
October 31, 2023
Glenn Henriksen photos October 29, 30 2023

Seasonal Change in Small Town Iowa

It was the first snowfall of wintertime
and whiteness spread around and on the black earth
falling from the heavenly clouds above
to cover once green lawns and fertile ground--
announcing the arrival of another season now beginning
which came as annual harvesting neared its end;
persons hoped a few more working days would be found.

It had been gray the day before,
yet had been brightened by the occasional sighting of a sugar maple
with fallen leaves littering the surrounding earthen floor;
fog swirled on flat reflective surfaces of a local lake;
our photographer missed little while driving his daily miles,
and found much on scenic byways at which to aim and a photo take,
to later post on Facebook to our amazement and smiles.

Traveling northwest as conditions on the roadways worsened,
while the moisture became heavier on city lawns and windward bark,
as wetness gathered on the leaves still clinging to the branches
and cold flakes became stuffed into spaces on needled shrubs;
it quickly melted from the pavement, drives, and pedestrian walkways,
though it stuck to automobile glass and surfaces, and building rooftops--
but through the moisture and roadway tracks people drove home safely.

Summer plants knew the season was over and trees shed their clothes
and frozen moisture lay sheltered where moving air no longer blows;
blanketing it lay amongst the brown grasses in a ditch,
melting away early on corners' curves and roadside banks;
rows of farming equipment had waited out the storm
in grove-sheltered make-do parking lots near fields' edges--
the farmers hoping to finish harvest when weather again turned warm.

James R. Ellerston
October 31, 2023
Glenn Henriksen, October 29, 2023

Mideast War Games Again

Brutal carnage restarted by an attack on a music festival;
Guns fired on young listeners in an open field;
Inhumanity continued with grenades thrown into shelters killing occupants within;
Shelter locations were not safe from attacks stirred by racial hatred;
No age group was exempt from firepower raining destruction and death.

Occupied multi-story apartment buildings crumbled under powerful bombing;
Power plants were destroyed so no electricity could be supplied to hospitals;
Death counts were in the thousands, so many children had died;
Doctors attempted miracle operations on crowded hallway floors;
Only flashlights of cell phones lit their skilled hands moving surgical knives.

Allies of the opposing sides were criticized in world media commentary;
Allies sought to send aid but had appeared uninvolved;
Allies finally sent supplies in U.N. convoys of trucks across the sands;
Allies al last opened borders for escaping hostages;
Allies governments were begged by families to bring their captive children home.

Two religions were again at war with each other's righteous beliefs;
Two ethnicities tried to kill the other for power and control;
Two self-entitled nations fought for the other's land and water;
Two militaries dreamed of bombing each other to oblivion;
Two sides medical teams struggled to keep wounded persons alive.

James R. Ellerston
November 2, 2023

Gift Of A Watermelon

A late summer's beautiful taste;
eagerly awaited, always satisfying;
succulent, sweet, wet, thirst quenching;
tasty, crisp, a crunchy texture at the right time;
when cold, so satisfying, this product from a family garden.

Soul relaxing, mind calming when chilled;
a result of nature's cultivation with water and hoe;
transportable pleasure, a gift of the generosity of a friend;
a perfect end to a day, something to share with others;
she had given me more than a watermelon from a family farm.

James R. Ellerston
November 3, 2023
Marge Gale had given me a melon and apples October 4, 2023

Thoughts About When I Walked On A Saturday Afternoon

This perfect walking day I moved around my usual concrete paths
when the temperature was warm and the sun was on my face;
thick grass was green across the stretches of campus lawn
and leaves in autumn faded yet clung upon the branch;
in afternoons I frequently walked this place so dear to me--
today on a day when crowds of youth explored our halls.

Young exploring scholars strode these connecting routes
while birds cried out from buildings' cornices and eves;
their calls sounded forth amid the silence of the low-key Saturday;
busy squirrels searched the ground beneath the oaks;
sunshine turned more golden while the hours passed away
as floating clouds moved slowly across a pale blue sky.

I sat down to rest upon a shaded mesh steel bench
outside doors to a building where I had once felt at home;
I heard student conversations pass me by and fade distantly away
and watched the man loading in equipment for an evening concert
which eventually found my ears in performance the following day
when musicians showed musical skills and were again applauded.

James R. Ellerston
November 4,5,6, 2023

A Morning Phone Call

The telephone call had come from Michigan in a somber tone
and reached us in Iowa on a cell phone with a message--
that the last of a family generation living in Illinois had died that day.

As of that day all of my wife's aunts had passed on and were gone;
Auntie Janie would no longer occupy her room and bed for daily life
in the place of rest she had lived during her past years.

After 93 years, this beautiful woman left her earthly realm
at a surprise time, unexpected by us all, without a hint death was imminent;
Janie, my wife's mother's brother's wife was loved by her family.

Auntie Janie was loved dearly, the last family of WWII era survivors,
leaving the next age group to truly be the older generation;
she'd been a person who always made you feel good about yourself.

We remember her from our forest vacation place in Wisconsin
where she lived in the remodeled cabin next door
in a wooded site on the shore of a small lake called Thomat.

Energetically she had cared for the original house throughout the years;
she built a carport and redecorated within between playing rounds of golf;
when there, attended the United Methodist Church in Medford, Wisconsin.

It was big holiday meals that were the most memorable events,
with all the relatives sitting around a large table or balancing trays;
the food was always good; recipes were old and traditional.

We would get together in Aurora at their house on Randall Road,
and later at the family homes of her sons and daughters;
we hope to meet with family gathered to celebrate her life.

James R. Ellerston November 6,8,10, 2023
Jane Matteson 1930, -- November 6, 2023
Shelley Best Ellerston Facebook Post November 7, 2023

It Didn't Always Mean Something When She Nodded

In venerable spaces where solemn echoes ring
Kris DeWild reigns, with music her offering,
In the halls of worship, where hymns softly soar,
On the benches she sits, with melody her core;
Her skills adept, her movements on keys of organ and piano glide,
Weaving hymns that silently in print reside;
Her fingers dance on harp and cello strings
Crafting tunes that float above congregations while everyone sings;
Dressed in classy garments for reverence, her presence was to gently demand,
A maestro of voices, she directs the choir when to sit and to stand.

Each accompaniment note she strikes, a whisper of grace
In the sanctuary worship space, her most cherished place;
In her stance, a portrait of kindness while she commands,
This conductor of voices, held faith in her hands;
Yet, once amidst a solemn funeral's gloom,
In the stillness of a service draped in grief's veil,
A chuckle escaped, piercing the room,
A laugh emanated between her lips, a human detail,
A fleeting pause in her poise and guise,
A moment's lapse from her composed facade,
Revealing her humanity, to no one's surprise.

For Kris, though usually proper and still,
Holds a heart that humor can easily fill,
Revealing a soul where lightness and depth are not at odds,
But in this contrast, her true essence is founded,
Within a blend of reverence and joy, her spirit is unbounded;
In this juxtaposition, her spirit thrives,
Between reverence and joy, her essence derives.

So in the church where handbell echoes resound,
In the steepled building where ancient hymn tunes sound,
Her music and energetic leadership profoundly abound;
Kris DeWild is a name etched in congregational lore,
She is a choir director, and so much more;
Between the changing tonalities and choral refrains,
One finds harmonies where sacredness actually remains;
Her legacy is in each phrase, breath taken, and silence heard,
In spaces among notes, between sacred sounds and the absurd.

James R. Ellerston November 11, 2023
Christopher M. Ellerston November 10, 2023
Assistance from the Artificial Intelligence Program for writing called Chat GPT
Kris DeWild has had a long career in Music Education and Sacred Music, and serves at Second Reformed Church in Pella, Iowa as organist, choir director, and bell choir director, and other leadership positions. She also plays viola, saxophone, and accordion.

"What Sweeter Music" Could Have Reached One's Ears

After my usual afternoon walk I heard their rehearsal
when I rested my body in a red padded auditorium seat,
while the sun descended in the clear western sky
and streaks of golden light shone through glass on hallowed walls.

Voices of this choir uplifted my being,
the beauty of their harmonies moved me emotionally;
lungs inhaled together and mouths produced tonal vowels
as young men and women shared the joy of singing together.

An energy of musical line propelled the students forward;
they sat and stood amid each other raising voices on life's stage;
suppressing individuality united into one focussed ensemble,
in singing music both familiar and newly-inspired.

Sacred and historical texts inspired personal musical efforts;
blended pitches showed balance with combined efforts of others;
soprano melodies floated above a solid foundation of bass voices;
alto and tenor sounds wove together our hearing experience.

All transpired under a masterful director's creative leadership
which left no questions about what should be attempted next--
things to be tried with united purpose to improve a performance--
to elevate their choral art to a higher place in human activities.

James R. Ellerston
November 14, 2023
Central College A Cappella Choir rehearsal November 13, 2023

In A Tuesday Afternoon Rehearsal

The wind players in the band were spread across the wide stage,
percussion instruments and percussionists encircled around the back;
an instructor stood front and center, stick in his hand;
a string bass player in shorts and athletic shoes stood near stage's edge.

Music playing started with metronome clicks and a batton wave;
trumpet riffs soared and woodwinds played scale-like passages;
rhythms were vocalized to emphasize accents and staccato;
the director's mantra was "get the tempo in your head".

A talented freshman stood poised by his upright instrument,
a cap in place on his head with the bill forward, as is his attitude;
thinking rhythms, the kid finds joy in the low notes he plunks out,
naturally anticipating the beat to make the tune swing.

The rehearsal is a model of using clocked time efficiently;
there is always attention to detail and performing with dynamics,
making pleasure and joy, and emotional involvement happen for the listener;
when the students play well, the conductor always compliments their efforts.

James R. Ellerston
November 15, 2023
SWE rehearsal in Douwstra Auditorium November 14, 2023
Brade Lampe is an instrumental music instructor at Central College, Pella IA
Freshman student Dominic Sexton plays string bass in bands and orchestra

Somme:
WWI Poems
From Letters I.-XII.

Somme: WWI Poems From Letters

I.

Just as dawn was breaking the 2nd of July we moved up the road
           past the now demolished barricade
across the old no-man's land
           and enemy's erstwhile front line
relieving some of the Norfolks in the trenches
           a short distance over;
after daylight, we were still a long way from the 'front'
           and were still in 'reserve';
…a look around the captured trenches,
           …literally smashed by our bombardment
…but few of the numerous dugouts were damaged
           …one with an entrance blown in.

German dead were everywhere, many being in dugouts
           …as if they had died there after being wounded in the trenches;
…most of those Germans who had been killed
           appeared to have died in the trenches;
along the remains of the parapet were little piles
           of empty cartridge cases where they had lain and fired;
in most cases the Germans lay on the bottom of the trenches
           …many having a bullet hole in the head;
stretcher bearers were searching the trenches among the dead
           for any who still had life in them.

II.

The third day I was exhausted, and it was on this day that a thunderstorm
	...broke the terrific heat--
by this time all the bodies around me
	had turned black;
one of them had a waterproof sheet protruding
	at the back of his pack--
I formed a ridge and the water trickled
	down into my mouth;
the fourth day was relatively quiet but I realized
	that my time was getting short,
and unless help arrived soon,
	I was finished;
I made my mind up that whatever happened,
	I must reach my lines by morning.

Crawling throughout the night I got to within a few yards
	of our trenches by daybreak;
by a sustained effort, I rose to my feet
	and hopped the necessary distance;
machine guns opened out but I held my course,
	lucky to enter a lane cut for the attack;
A sentry shouted "Who's there?"
	I croaked "Koyli";
To hear my own tongue being spoken--
	it was nectar;
"And yours?"
	"Middlesex" came the reply;
"Anyone else out there?"
	I told him "No".

III.

We were wondering what we could do
        to get the flood out of our trench
when we saw two or three Jerries climb onto the parapet of their trench
        and start digging with those long-handled shovels of theirs;
they must have seen us because as the water
        came pouring out of their trench
one of them lifted the blade of his shovel into the air
        and waved a 'washout'.

I at once gave them the same signal
        with the butt of my rifle;
it seemed to me that this was an event that was apart
        from the ordeal and enmity of battle;
the forces of nature had restored
        the sense of common humanity
after all the carnage there had been
        since the battle started.

Not a shot was fired on either side
        while we stood in danger of being drowned.

IV.

We are right back in a place Amiens
        bathed in the deepest summer peace;
No sound of the guns
        reach us here--
behind this farm, among its big trees
        is a charming garden;
Madonna lilies and roses mix with onions and peas,
        rosemary and potatoes,
pinks and turnips, currants, and strawberries
        all jostle each other;
this afternoon all was basking in the sunshine,
        a fresh breeze stirred the trees;
there was a pleasant accompaniment of birds' songs
        and farmyard sounds.

On one side of the garden was an orchard;
        some red cows, ready for milking, were eagerly grazing
across the old pasture
        where long shadows fell;
rich fields of corn lay around the farm
        and in the near valley
between the woods on high ground opposite;
        there a little church stood up;
far away across the Somme, miles of unbroken fields
        sloped up to the horizon
with here and there a dark clump of trees
        or a distant wood;
utter and most refreshing peace and beauty
        brooded over the whole.

V.

There was comfort in coming straight from the trenches to a billet
        where a fire was always at our disposal for warmth or cuisine;
this to be compared with a return to an empty hut
        with coke braziers and canvas partitions to retain some warmth;
there was need to replace a friendly children and mother interaction
        in a half-hour 'round the fire before going to bed;
to create an atmosphere of mental change and recreation so needed
        during the months of continuous warfare.

Military pay was of little use to the men with only limited supplies
        at a divisional canteen available to them;
long winter evenings were spent herded together in huts
        with flickering candle light for writing, game, or nap;
outside were no village walks on avenues of trees with happy life
        no movement for all to see but only mud for transport;
there were struggling efforts going to and fro;
        or cross a hundred yards sinking deep in liquid mud.

VI.

The battalion was withdrawn to a camp after many days in the trenches
        November rains had stopped and the men went foraging;
spirits rose appreciably and companies built their own bonfires
        as if in recognition of our display of self help the rain stopped;
the scene had changed from guys drooping dejectedly
        talking in undertones;
men regained their spirits and energy and laughter
        and songs rose from the circles around the fires.

VII.

What silly details my letters must seem
            to give you dear home people
who are looking for big results
            and moves of miles by army corps;
they cannot realize as we can and do what it means
            to gain even a short length of the enemy's front line trench;
what organization, what preparation, what buzzing
            of thousands of Morse messages over the phone or by lamps.

We may not get your letters for a week now,
            though you'll get ours;
I washed my hands in my mess tin
            with a cupful of water--
otherwise I could not have written,
            being plastered with mud;
water is a jewel of rarity-- a two mile walk each way
            through the communication trench to fetch it.

The greatest difficulty is dealing with the badly wounded;
            this morning a man had his leg torn from his thigh to ankle;
it is very awkward to carry such cases out, poor beggars,
            the labor is enormous, almost killing to the stretcher bearers;
I helped to carry a man across the open for a short mile
            and shall never forget it;
here it is over two miles of torturous trench--
            slipping and inches of mud at that.

Dead silence has rent the air
            for the last ten minutes;
the rain is so thick
            no observing can take place;
there is an earth-trembling sort of rumble
            that shows there is heavy firing going on somewhere;
any chance of strafing heavily up or down the line bucks you up
            and makes you think we shall finish them off before Christmas.

VIII.

Someone was asking if there was to be a sort of Christmas truce
           and he was glad to say there is not;
strict orders have been issued there is to be no such waste of kindness
           toward an enemy causing us many losses by foulest means;
we are spending five million pounds a day on the war
           and every day makes it harder for the Germans;
why waste five millions and slacken the awful tanking they are getting?
           we want them fed up, not give opportunities for feeding up;
if they send a shell or two over to our infantry trenches on Christmas Day--
           as they most certainly will--
we are to respond with a searching unceasing bombardment of their trenches
           that will break up their Christmas parties.

IX.

The last evening being cold, innumerable small fires of brushwood and twigs
           were lit all over the field
and around these the men sprawled
           in attitudes of ease
while some sang and were merry, others gave themselves
           to talk of the yesterdays and tomorrows,
or were silent in the presence of the surge of memories or hoped for things
           they saw limned in the red heart of the fire;
the spectacle of that gloomy field with its twinkling fires,
           figures of the men moving about in dark silhouette
against the soft and varied radiances
           lives in the memory;
for many, so sadly many of these good fellows--
           were destined not to outlive the morrow.

X.

Later in the morning we Suffolks had been moved forward
> in case we were needed;

in the early afternoon the enemy's shelling
> gradually died down;

we past along one of the 'Assembly' trenches, heavily shelled by the enemy,
> apparently during the morning;

several of our men were lying dead in it,
> killed by the enemy's shells;

in one place a man was kneeling, as if in prayer,
> his hands covering his face;

lying in the trench behind him was another man face downwards,
> half-buried in the earth, thrown into the trench by the shells;

another man was sitting on the firestep, buried to the knees,
> looking as if he had be,een suddenly turned to stone;

further along I slipped, and looking down saw a piece of a man's backbone,
> and pieces of flesh strewn about;

hanging down from the parapet was a mass of entrails,
> already swarming with flies;

we finally took up a position astride the road--
> the enemy's guns were now quite quiet.

XI.

As a battalion, we tramped the old duckboards again yesterday afternoon;
        as of now we've got two companies in the front line;
outside it is snowing gently;
        there is wrath and recrimination within;
after carrying a rum jar right up here, somebody set it down on a stone,
        and the earth has drunk most of the rum;
the men cannot forget the tragedy, only the strong odor pervades the place;
        they are not content with smell instead of taste;
two days of duckboard tramping carrying wire, stakes, rations, and bombs,
        left little time for town before being readied back to the line;
I am tired, physically and mentally tired;
        leave deferred maketh the heart sick--
sick of the energy of those belching guns firing over our heads
        as we tramp the never-ending duckboards.

XII.

This 16th of January the cold is intense--
        the wind of a bitterness indescribable;
the worst of it is that the frost here always means a mist
        which makes shooting very difficult;
things have quieted down as far as infantry action is concerned,
        but both sides still bombard each other pretty hard;
we don't get much rest-- in addition to fighting by day we have to shoot
        from 6pm to 6:00 am every second night, a long cold business;
the are giving me two more howitzers--making me up to a six gun battery
        which will be rather nice.

James R. Ellerston
November 17, 22, 2023
Based on letters and writings by actual soldiers that were quoted

From the following sources:
The Somme: The Epic Battle In The Soldiers' Own Words and Photographs
compiled by Richard van Emden published by Pen and Sword Military an imprint of Pen and Sword
Books Ltd., 47 Church Street, Barnsley, South Yorkshire S70 2AS UK
Copyright Richard van Emden 2016   356 pages   ISBN 1473885175
The offensive on the Somme took place between July and November 1916

I.
Page 153, Private Sydney Fuller; 8th Suffolk Regiment

II.
Page 156, Sergeant Walter Popple; 8th King's Own Yorkshire Light Infantry

III.
Page 157, Sergeant Charles Moss, 18th Battalion Durham Light Infantry

IV.
Page 161, Captain Harold Bidder, 1st South Staffordshire Regiment

V.
Pages 308, 309, Captain Eric Whitworth, 12th South Wales Borderers

VI.
Pages 309, 310, Captain Sidney Rogerson, 2nd West Yorkshire Regiment

VII.
Pp. 38-40 Gunner Cecil Longley, 1st Sth. Midland Brig. Royal Field Artillery

VIII.
Page 48, Gunner Cecil Longley, 1st Sth. Midland Brig. Royal Field Artillery

IX.
Pages 163, 164, Private Thomas Lyon, 1/9th Highland Light Infantry

X.
Pages 136, 137, Private Sydney Fuller: 8th Suffolk Regiment

XI.
Pages 323, 324, Lieutenant Max Plowman, 10th West Yorkshire Regiment

XII.
Page 325, Major Cuthbert Lawson, 14th Brigade Royal Horse Artillery

Thanksgiving
For Fall Harvest
Done

Five November Happenings

I.

Trees drop their once green summer growth now browning;
Leaves litter near lifeless drying lawns;
Delivery people are overworked and seasonally burdened;
Packages crowd front porch corners in sliding stacks.

II.

Post boxes fill-up with happy holiday greetings;
Christmas cards cross wide distances between friends;
Merry messages are opened with great joy;
Arriving presents create thankful anticipation.

III.

Dancing dogs are bouncing and barking at windows' panes;
Energetic announcements of parcel arrivals;
Mailboxes stuffed with bills, charity requests, and ads;
A napping man sleeps away the hours of the afternoon.

IV.

Coffee beans brew mornings' beakers of beverage;
Toast browning but not burning awaits spreading butter;
Eggs are frying until whites are solid and yolks hardened;
Sizzling bacon awakes appetites slowly.

V.

Flaming long logs burn on the home hearth ablaze;
A flickering fire adds cheer and welcome warmth
On a cold cloudy early winter windy week
When we are housebound from the chill for dismal days.

James R. Ellerston   November 18, 2023

His Harvest Of 2023 Corn Completed

A giant harvester had moved through the final field;
the last rows of corn were combined
under blue skies with wispy white clouds,
the green tractor pulling the wagon alongside
as the cornhead cut through outside rows near the fence.

Ground-up stalks were spread out the rear of the machine
and scattered evenly on the ground;
rows of corn stubble stretched toward horizons;
shadows played across the harvested yellow fields
in late afternoon with its golden light from a descending sun.

The nearly last and final loads of corn came into town,
both by tractor and semi-truck
and were taken to the elevator in Ringsted;
it was the end of a safe and bountiful crop year,
always a good time for farmers when their harvest is in.

Plowing could be done beginning another day;
low and yet strong sun's rays
shone brightly in the late afternoon hours,
above a western horizon and in spaces between farm grove trees;
from open pods milkweed seeds floated away on gentle breezes.

He drove home past a harvested field in his car
with numerous cornstalk bales-- a pretty sight
reminding one of old-fashioned corn shocks of yesteryear;
it's amazing how the cattle still found stuff
to eat from the outside of the giant round bales.

In between hauling loads he stopped to view a homestead--
his great grandparents place near Ringsted;
the farm was once a showplace,
but now is in disrepair with only a few outbuildings,
plus four imposing concrete silos banded with steel rings.

If the ancient cottonwoods around the Ringsted farm could talk--
they would tell history of being probably planted in 1882;
actually the trees do 'talk' with their heart-shaped flat leaves
when they flutter in response to the Iowa winds blowing--
a sound loved by those living on this farm.

Later he stopped by graves in a nearby cemetery,
seeing the monument stones of his great grandparents
whose resting place is just a half mile away
from the farm where they homesteaded in 1882
after immigrating from Denmark in the year 1880.

While he drove, there were still spots of icy snow
remaining in the north sloping bottoms of ditches,
across from the corn fields and in town;
a little white snow remained in peaceful contrast
on the north roof of an Armstrong park shelter house.

James R. Ellerston
November 22, 2023
Photos, writings of Glenn Henriksen November 1,2,6,7,21, 2023
Comments Nov. 2nd, 6th, Sara Vriesen; Nov. 6th, LaVonne Tow

After The Fall Harvest

Dry leaves laid thickly on his town property in the morning;
a little white-painted barn was surrounded by fallen silver maple leaves,
with the ash trees behind bereft of leaves.

He is V-ripping soybean stubble, extending his afternoon into evening,
while he was privileged to take in another fantastic sunset
from his glass-surrounded tractor cab.

A day before he'd seen a sunset turn into night as he plowed a cornfield
with dark tree groves well silhouetted against the orange-hued heavens;
black Iowa soil emerged from a 5 bottom moldboard plow turning the earth.

An old abandoned corncrib granary sat poignantly at sunset,
sheltering an old truck awaiting restoration
parked in its center in between the cribs.

He brought back to his farm a conventional plowing method on corn stubble,
hoping a moldboard plow would 'freshen' soils after minimal tillage methods;
this plowed land was protected by windbreaks to protect it from erosion.

A farm boy growing up on deep plowing tillage he enjoyed seeing black loam,
and catching the smell of the freshly turned blackness;
his appreciation was enhanced for the richness of this resource.

Sometimes seagulls would follow you when plowing;
they come right-up next to you just out of reach and pace you for a bit;
birds would often find worms before they took off.

One night he saw a sunset from all directions in his vision with many colors
driving inside a glass-surrounded place of warmth seeing beautiful designs,
thanking the Lord for his eyes with which to see this beauty.

James R. Ellerston November 20, 2023
Photos and comments of Glenn Henricksen
Comments by Mark Grabinoski, Sara Vriesen

Moving Toward Thanksgiving

Southwest of his hometown the river was low between and in its banks;
dried grasses stood tall, waving in the winds at sunset;
limbs of riverbank trees scraped bare against the heavens;
roadside cedars stood strongly toward the sky;
utility poles stretched their wires along roadside ditches.

Dusty roads and angus cattle made for memorable visual scenes;
on a ride in Iowa he saw horses grazing along a fence near his farm;
wooden posts in a line climbed the hill upward behind them;
reaching into the blue sky, craggy trees grew on hillsides;
orange and brown oak leaves were in view on and off their trees.

Late afternoon shadows lay across golden fields of corn stalks,
light made stripes on green grass among trees in a farm grove
where a curious cat prowled a family farmstead;
yellow sunlight silhouetted spruce trees against the clouds
and lit up the bark of trees along a gravel driveway.

He loves the warm November sunshine glow
as the sun readies to set at the farm;
in words and sounds he makes music out of visual experiences of nature;
he finds fun in seeing straight rows of hundreds of seagulls sitting,
feeding on worms from a farmer's fresh plowing as he continued his work.

November's fall colors are darker and more muted for the most;
and he loves the contrast of dark and light together under a cloudy sky;
drying grasses sway viewing across a field to timber stands above the river;
bird nests, mushrooms, and lichen provided details on branches and trunks;
a single red maple leaf lies upon the green grass.

Clustered drying oak leaves lie among leaves scattered near a foundation;
even the smallest gooseberry shrub vies for attention to its rich colors;
wildflower colors are in bloom amidst the remaining green grasses;
a single cottonwood tree is seen across a tilled field against an orange sky;
trees stand stalwart in a grove at the cemetery near the town of Armstrong.

James R. Ellerston November 20, 21, 2023
Photos and comments of Glenn Henricksen November 18, 19, 20, 2023
Comment of Carol and Dave Platt and Karma Ibsen and Sara Vriesen

Sixty Years Afterward There Is No Debate About Some Facts

At a thrift store I had bought a beautiful blue and white Wedgewood plate
commemorating the Apollo moon landing and moonwalk,
so I sent a picture of it proudly to my friend;
but he replied, "the fake moon landing";
I had written back, "I believe it was real!". Walter Cronkite had said so.

Despite the passing of six decades since that Nov. 22nd in Dallas,
we all remember where we were when we heard the news;
pain, confusion and a forever sadness wondering why, followed us in life;
school students stayed home nationwide the next days,
staring at black and white television images for hours in disbelief.

Definitive pictures marked our childhood or adolescence with memories,
our lives would never have the same optimism again;
but we did go to the surface of the moon within his promised decade;
but while some still think it was a faked performance for TV
and in reality, never had happened, in actual fact it had occurred.

While my family was in a lakeshore cabin we watched on an 11 inch TV;
that evening as brave men strode across the lunar soil and dust;
and a full moon floated in silver-white glory in the sky over my beloved lake;
I am a dreamer of dreams and believed what the young President had said;
I am still a believer that men did walk there in fact like he said they would.

James R. Ellerston
November 23, 2023
Reply to Facebook Messenger comment by Stefan Crowl on Nov. 22, 2023
President J.F. Kennedy was assassinated in Dallas, Texas Nov. 22, 2023

I Mourned With Ireland

This week I mourned along with Ireland,
such thoughts dominated me the remainder of that week--
watching on my cell phone the videos for days--
hearing the music of the late musician--
the recently deceased Shane MacGowan;
his lyrics moving our minds to better understand our humanity
with melodies and music now causing so many to tear.

On streaming videos I stood in Dublin's streets with Irish people--
large crowds on pavements lining both curbs so very early--
for a glimpse of the horse drawn stately hearse,
and through glass to see a wicker casket draped with Ireland's flag;
my heart sang out with the lyrics of his beloved Christmas tune
as I listened to the hordes sing out his most famous songs;
and a young piper sat next to a driver guiding four black horses.

In Tipperary at his funeral-- some wrapped in quilted winter coats,
and against bitter breezes wearing stocking caps upon their heads,
overflow crowds stood outside the big Catholic church with coffin within,
people out there who could not find room within the building;
one held the Irish standard high; it was blowing in the brisk wind;
others standing in a silent crowd listened respectfully, heads bowed,
while flags and a requested Budha were carried honorably inside.

All over the nation, in Ireland's many bars and on concert stages
music this man had written was loudly, proudly sung out--
and a Christmas "fairy tale" song from years ago
climbed the Ireland and UK pop music charts each day;
within that church sacred sacraments were said and prayers pronounced,
and singers sang his lyrics and people danced out of their pews;
all this near his wicker casket, "and bells rang out on Christmas Day".

James R. Ellerston
December 12, 2023
Shane MacGowan was a member of the band Pogues.
His funeral was December 7, 2023

Check Out James R. Ellerston's Other Books Available on Amazon

Between Two Covers Some Lives Are Secure [2022]
ISBN: 9798365903326

Surely, It's Poetry Time [2022]
ISBN: 9798793522113

Dream — But Do Not Make Dreams Your Master [2021]
ISBN: 9798587710788

These Hastily Scribbled Thoughts Convey My Inner Soul [2020]
ISBN: 9788640035803

Sing in Me, Oh Muse, and Through Me Tell the Story [2019]
ISBN: 9781088772683

Weaving the Tapestry of Life: A Book of Poetry [2019]
ISBN: 9781793959614

Look to the Interests of Others [2018]
ISBN: 9781981559343

Newer Thoughts, Older Musings [2017]
ISBN: 9781544277226

Thoughts, Meditations, and Songs [2016]
ISBN: 9781523345663

The Winds Have Freshened, the Sails Are Full: A Collection [2016]
ISBN: 9781530579709

Like People, These Are Not Meant to Stand Alone [2015]
ISBN: 9781511575669

Events of Time Through Life's History in Poems: 1963-2015 [2015]
ISBN: 9781518894503

La Grande Guerre: Writings Before and After the Armistice (1918-1919) [2015]
ISBN: 9781505618501

Poems from Travels in Three Countries: A Collection [2014]
ISBN: 9781500522476

Finishing and Publishing by Keegan Joël VanDevender

Keegan Joël VanDevender is an educator, linguist and world traveler, and lifelong learner from Pella, Iowa. He is an educator, specializing in English, language arts, journalism, Spanish, and teacher education. He earned a bachelor's degree (B.A.) in Secondary English/Language Arts and Journalism Education from William Penn University (Oskaloosa, Iowa); a master's degree (M.Ed.) in Curriculum, Instruction, and Teacher Leadership with an emphasis in Technology Integration from Buena Vista University (Storm Lake, Iowa); a post-graduate certificate in Spanish Education from Fort Hays State University (Hays, Kansas); and is currently pursuing a doctorate (Ph.D.) in Education at Drake University (Des Moines, Iowa) and a second master's degree in educational administration from Northwestern College (Orange City, Iowa). His research interests include active learning strategies in a blended/hybrid learning environment, teacher education/preparation programming, as well as the implementation of standards-based grading (SBG) in post-secondary settings such as undergraduate teacher education programs.

Made in the USA
Monee, IL
15 January 2024